HD9940.U42 P38 2007

Paul, Gerald,

My business life cycle :
how innovation,
    c2007.

My Business Life Cycle

My Business Life Cycle

How Innovation, Evolution, and Determination Made Paul Harris Great

by Gerald Paul

with Victoria Barrett

Purdue University Press / West Lafayette, Indiana

Printed in the United States of America.

ISBN 978-1-55753-426-2
      1-55753-426-8

Library of Congress Cataloging-in-Publication Data
Paul, Gerald, 1924-
    My business life cycle : how innovation, evolution, and determi-
nation made Paul Harris great / by Gerald Paul.
        p. cm.
    ISBN 978-1-55753-426-2 (alk. paper)
    1. Paul, Gerald, 1924-   2. Harris Paul Retail Stores, Inc.--
History.   3. Businesspeople--United States--Biography.   4. Cloth-
ing trade--United States. 5. Fashion merchandising--United States.
I. Title.
    HD9940.U42P38 2007
    381'.45687092--dc22
    [B]
                                                    2006038907

Dedicated to my wife, Dorit,

who was my constant and steadfast support,
counselor, and adviser
during the many years Paul Harris was developing.

CONTENTS

FOREWORD

You certainly have heard of Sam Walton. You may not know who J.C. Penney was, but you know there is a chain of stores with his name on it. You may have heard of Stanley Marcus (founder of Neiman Marcus), Mary Kay Ash (Mary Kay), Jeff Bezos (Amazon.com), Richard Sears, A. Montgomery Ward, Marshall Field, Les Wexner (The Limited). You may have even have heard of Gordon Segal, founder of Crate and Barrel, and Bernard Marcus, the founder of Home Depot. But you probably have not heard of Gerald Paul. Even so, his story is as compelling, interesting, and educational as any of the other historical figures in retailing.

The chain of retail stores bearing his name is gone. But his place in retail history and his influence are not. His achievements are as much the great American Dream as is Sam Walton's. In fact his story and success may more sharply etch what can happen to all of us. The success of Sam Walton in building the largest retail company in the world was as much a surprise to him as anyone in the 1950s and 60s. No one could have predicted, or did predict that success. Part genius, part luck, part being in the right place in the right time with the right idea with the right execution. While none of us will become Sam Walton and build the largest chain of stores in the world, we can all become Gerald Paul.

This does not minimize his success and his legacy. Far from it. Most of us do not reach his level of success and influence. Yet we can. The American Dream: emigrate, work hard, look for opportunities, build a business, earn enough money to live comfortably, raise a family, and give back to your community. At some level we all want to be Gerald and Dorit Paul.

Retailers come and go, and their success is not based on living forever. Retailers are not made to live forever. Many start. Few live for 20 years. Very few build a chain of 360 stores, the size of Paul Harris at its largest. Only a handful ever have sales of 300 million dollars. Wal-Mart may seem invincible now, but 20 years from now, there may be someone else. In the 1980s, when Sears was the number-one retail chain, no one predicted that they would almost go out of business and have to merge with K-Mart for any chance of survival. The retail landscape is littered by names and stores that no longer exist: Montgomery Ward, Allied Stores, LS Ayres, Blocks, Gimbels, B. Altman's, Wanamakers, and on and on.

Paul Harris Stores did exactly what it was supposed to. It brought fashion, comfort, style, and functionality to millions of women in the Midwest. Midwestern women did not have to go to New York City to get fashion; they could go to their mall in Ohio and Indiana. Gerald Paul made women look good and feel good, and in doing so helped them craft their entry into the workplace leadership roles they now find themselves in. He understood what women wanted to wear and was able to make that vision real. Paul Harris's run of 50 years is remarkable because so few retail stores make it that long and so few make it so big. Paul Harris Stores was what I call a little giant. It made malls possible because malls could not exist on Big Stores alone; they needed little specialty stores to fill in and attract customers. Paul Harris Stores was part of the growth of specialty retailing that still accounts for 40 percent or so of all retail business.

Gerald Paul's life and his experiences tell us so much about U.S. culture, retail history, and a brand of entrepreneurship that appears to be making a comeback at our universities and schools and is seen most clearly in the growth of e-retailing. The story of Gerald Paul and Paul Harris Stores is instructive for any businessperson and for any retailer. If we do not learn from the past we are destined to relive the mistakes of those who went before us. As we read the history of Paul Harris Stores we see the decisions and steps for success and can apply them to any business we might find ourselves in. As we read Gerald Paul's story we also see a story of dreams and individual accomplishment that many of us might be only able to imagine. It is a story of possibilities: that is The Great American Story.

The Paul Harris story is a traditional American story of entrepreneurship, hard work, risk taking. It is a story of trial and error, of working as hard as you can towards a goal. It is a story of giving back to people and community. Gerald and Dorit Paul are in some ways everyday people; if you passed them on the street you might not even notice. But sit down and talk to them and you begin to see how their experience and their commitments to life illustrate how ordinary people can do extraordinary things, and help others to, as well.

Gerald Paul's legacy is in the millions of satisfied customers, many of whom still wear Paul Harris clothing years after the chain no longer exists. His legacy rests with the hundreds, yes hundreds, of retail professionals and executives who received their start or their retail experience at Paul Harris. His legacy rests with the thousands of employees who over the years were able to earn a living. His legacy rests in the State of Indiana, which has benefited from the generosity of Gerald and his wife and partner, Dorit. His legacy rests with the students at Purdue University, who are better people and professionals because they were in one of his classes. In every way his legacy is as strong and interesting as any of the other retail and business leaders you may have heard of. You may not have heard of Gerald Paul, but if you visit Indianapolis the art and culture is in part a result of the economic generosity, the generosity of spirit and effort of Gerald and Dorit Paul (made possible by the success of Paul Harris Stores). You may not have heard of Paul Harris Stores, but go to any mall and look at any specialty store. It is because of chains like Paul Harris and retail geniuses like Gerald Paul that we have an abundance of choice for the common woman (and man). You may not have heard of Gerald Paul and Paul Harris Stores, but many of the executives of those stores that you visit may have gotten their start or significant experience in his company. You may not have heard of Gerald Paul or his chain of stores, but the specialty stores of today, whether they know it or not, stand on the shoulders of retail executives like Gerald Paul and retail stores like Paul Harris.

Richard Feinberg, Ph.D.
Professor of Retail Management
Director, Center for Customer Driven Quality
Purdue University

My Business Life Cycle

Prologue

"To exist is to change. To change is to mature. To mature is to go on creating oneself endlessly."

ON A FALL DAY IN 1954, Gerald Paul stood in an empty storeroom with his business partner, Earl Harris. Gerald had a vision for the future. They would build something enduring, something inventive. It would be bigger than either of them, would outlive them. Right here, in a strip shopping center in Plainfield, Indiana, they would start the rest of their lives.

Paul Harris Stores was born in that strip center of ingenuity and drive. The partners kept their store open until nine at night, provided air-conditioning and free parking—all customer-service novelties. Both men kept their day jobs and ran the store at night; both invested everything they had.

Gerald and Earl had different dreams. Earl had a large family to support; as long as the company did well, he was fulfilled. But Gerald Paul was driven by something else. He could never have been happy with one successful 3,000-square-foot retail store. He always wanted something he hadn't imagined yet.

For forty years, he pushed the company to evolve and grow at every opportunity. It seems, after all, to have been the evolution, the change itself, that propelled Gerald forward; each achievement was, above all else, a springboard to the next thing. "To exist is to change" was his and the company's motto. Throughout the organization, everyone knew that change was the order of each day, that welcoming and initiating change were the keys to Paul Harris's success. Gerald Paul made sure they knew—this motto peppers company documents and human resources brochures; it was invoked in

formal meetings and casual conversations. It had real meaning for
Paul Harris's leaders and employees, and produced great benefits
for the chain's customers.

This urgent pursuit of the new produced a special kind of corporate culture: a culture of change. It didn't matter if it was one
store with five employees or three hundred stores with many, many
employees; everyone knew that their creativity and drive were essential to the company's evolution. For Paul Harris employees, this
meant different things. Some saw a place where women were far
more comfortable than men. Some relished the chance to use their
creativity. But for every single person I've talked with, it fostered a
fierce loyalty to the company and to its leader, Gerald Paul. They
described vast wells of admiration for their former boss and their
friend. His impression on the people involved with Paul Harris has
lived beyond their employment and beyond the life of the company
itself.

Gerald Paul's drive to succeed and his belief that he and his
company could always do better were both contagious and unflap-
pable. He shared with the people in his company an emotional bond,
and a strong pride in the work they did and the organization they
built. Through disasters of natural, financial, and personnel variet-
ies, Gerald saw opportunities to grow the organization and to grow
as an individual.

His leadership produced a remarkable company. The first store
quickly doubled in size. Before long, stores popped up all around
Indianapolis. At its peak, Paul Harris was a focused women's clothing retailer with more than 300 stores. It was a staple in the fashion
diet of many stylish women.

Each time the company grew, its leaders faced a wide range of
risks. Earl Harris worried that changes were going to jeopardize
the company's success. But Gerald was persistent, and at each major
turning point, his passion for building a great business, his energetic embrace of challenges, and his forward-thinking assessment
of each situation won out.

From the foundation of that Plainfield store in 1954 to the day
Gerald Paul retired in 1993, Paul Harris's people continued to take
risks. They saw the retail industry change. They sold clothing to
women before, during, and after the movement that brought them

out of the home and into the workplace. They faced bankruptcy re-organization alongside dozens of other retail companies in 1991; they faced reorganization with their heads up and eyes open and emerged healthy and wise.

The company made ill-informed changes, too. A breakneck-speed expansion helped lead the way into that bankruptcy. Difficult personnel decisions became consequential mistakes. But through four decades of fashion, Paul Harris thrived.

How does one "go on creating oneself endlessly"? Even more diffi-cult, how does one go on recreating a company endlessly? As Amer-ican businesses have come to recognize this need, "change manage-ment" has become a topic you can study in a business course or hire a consultant to teach. But in its very phrasing, "change man-agement" implies that change is inherently problematic, danger-ous, threatening. It means that change is inevitable and that, as a manager, you're going to have to find a way to keep it from wreck-ing your company. It works to encourage an embrace of change, like taking in a stranger at your front door, an unpredictable guest who might be scary, threatening, and difficult, or whose tenure in your home might be a blessing.

To talk about the culture of an organization, one has to con-sider endless variables. Every decision a leader makes can affect the workplace, image, and customer relationship. More importantly, a leader's attitude, passion, and commitment to the success of an or-ganization must be understood by his employees. Some of the spe-cific components of a specialty retailer's corporate culture revolve around equally abstract concepts: creativity, image, adaptability.

The retail industry is constantly changing, trying to keep up with the ever-changing consumer. As with any organization, a re-tailer can decide whether to resist change: Henry Ford said, "Give the public any color it wants as long as it is black." Fashion retailers, on the other hand, market an image. How does a woman see her-self? Does she wish to reshape her style to suit a retailer who sells French chic or outdoors rugged? Paul Harris believed that its con-sumer wished to buy clothes that reflected her existing self-image, clothes she could wear comfortably in many settings. As American culture changed, Gerald Paul and his company marketed clothes that women could wear in their emerging business careers. They focused further to offer items that let women be simultaneously feminine and professional. They made a regular practice of refining their focus to anticipate and exceed the expectations of their customers. Gerald and his employees believed that this practice required not just a process of rethinking and revision, but a forward-looking, pervasive enjoyment of change, an attitude more than a set of activities.

A culture of change is one in which the key players are always thinking on their feet. A project, if long in span, might die before its implementation. Hundreds of new ideas might be examined and discarded before one hits the mark. As CEO and chief merchandiser, it was Gerald Paul's passion to lead the development of this culture. He has always held change and reinvention as hallmarks of emotional and professional maturity. The right people for Paul Harris Stores, Inc. embraced this philosophy, too. Gerald believed, and he helped other people to believe, that stagnation would be the death of the company, and that a reverence for and excitement about constant change was the only way to survive.

Through the embrace of ongoing evolution, focus, and re-focus, Gerald Paul's leadership both exemplified and fulfilled his drive to constantly reach new heights.

The chief executive officer of a company is responsible for setting up an environment that determines how freely change is embodied. Gerald Paul didn't practice "change management." By the example of his own practices and, more importantly, his attitude and drive, he taught people to see change as opportunity: specifically, the opportunity for increased sales and profits, and for self-fulfillment through professional achievement and experience.

As the person responsible for Paul Harris Stores, Inc.'s merchandise decisions, Gerald knew early that to achieve the company's goal of becoming a focused specialty retailer recognized as an outstanding performer, he not only had to welcome and embrace change—change in tastes, change in markets—he had to see it coming. To succeed at this, he had to ensure that ideas could come forth freely. In this aspect, he became a *disorganizer*. With a staff of buyers, he traveled the world to bring new ideas home; he worked with vendors in China before U.S.-Chinese diplomacy was established. He learned to see each problem as an opportunity for personal and professional growth, to the advantage of the company. Always, at the center, was the customer. Paul Harris never sought to dictate a woman's image, but to reflect it. What moved Paul Harris forward was an understanding of the customer and a series of research projects—a spirit of inquiry—to enrich, redefine, and reinforce that understanding. Paul Harris was certainly not the first specialty retailer to commission and implement customer studies, but it was at the forefront. Research and testing, staying educated, and keeping the board of directors staffed with retail experts and university professors were all part of the culture of change. The majority of new ideas will not stand the test of examination and will be discarded, but systematizing that testing and encouraging the new ideas of all the company's players let the truly great inspirations float to the top.

How did Gerald Paul systematize evolution? He did his best to listen and to honor other people's knowledge. He made the customer his boss through research-driven processes. He invited consultants and subordinates to pick apart his leadership techniques. He enrolled in what was to become a groundbreaking Harvard study that helped Gerald understand himself better and was a major step in his development as a leader. And he *liked* change—sometimes to the despair of some employees. No matter what the company was doing, Gerald always asked if there was a better way.

The same passion for change that built Paul Harris Stores also blazed trails around the world for a man who devoted his life to growth. Gerald Paul's path from immigration as a teenager to escape Hitler to becoming a celebrated art collector and philanthropist in his Indianapolis hometown can't be separated from his visionary career at Paul Harris. The art collection and the devotion to art that so many in Indianapolis hold up as exemplary began on a business trip to Italy in 1954. The dedication to education that benefits Purdue University students every fall was fostered within the business. Gerald Paul drove himself to growth, creativity, and change with the same passion he applied to his company, and he made his company a vehicle for his own edification. Again and again, he made great things out of supplies another builder would have judged too small.

It doesn't matter that nothing remains of the company Gerald Paul built. This is still a story of great achievements, great challenges, and a great life. It's the story of a man who, like so many of us, wanted to build something larger than himself—who, in succeeding, became someone his friends and employees say they're lucky to know, someone whose life we should all learn from in our own longing for evolution.

—Victoria Barrett

CHAPTER ONE

Beginnings

MY STORY STARTS IN WITTEN, GERMANY, a town of 100,000 people, where my mother's family had lived for several generations. I started in public school at age six and at age ten transferred to a "Realgymnasium," which was semi-private and a quite rigorous school. When Hitler came to power in 1933, children of Jews were banned from the school unless their fathers had been officers in the German Army during World War I. Luckily, my father qualified, so I was permitted to remain in the school with only one other Jewish boy.

There were problems, of course. We had a teacher who always wore his Nazi uniform to class, including a long dagger hanging from his belt. He loved to call on me with the toughest questions, and if I didn't know the answer, he gave me lashes with a cane in front of the class. Every spring the entire class went for a week to a North Sea island, but Jews were not permitted to go, so I had to stay home. These and similar incidents influenced my early school years. This was in 1938; Hitler was making normal life impossible there, so my father arranged for us to leave Germany and come to America.

We were among the last families to be able to take possessions with us when we left Germany. All our belongings were packed into a wooden lift, a huge shipping crate. When it arrived by ship in New York, my father had trouble getting it to Indianapolis. It was too big for a truck and had to be put on a railroad car. When it arrived and was unpacked, it was sold and became a garage for someone; the local newspaper ran a photo of it.

I was a boy of thirteen when we came to the United States from Germany. We came to Indianapolis because we had relatives in the city. Everything was new, and I understood almost no English. Our relatives in Indianapolis spoke only English and were strangers to me. It would be a difficult new beginning.

The very next day after we arrived in Indianapolis, two of my aunts took me to Shortridge High School to enroll me in summer school. Of course, since we couldn't communicate well, I was quite lost. In class, it was as though they were speaking Chinese: I couldn't understand a word. I was terribly frustrated. I would get home and cry and didn't think I'd ever learn the language. But some people were very nice to me. I remember a girl who would draw a tree on a piece of paper and say "tree" and I would say, "tree." Step-by-step, I gradually learned what was going on in class. It required a great amount of patience and energy.

Along with school, I went to English classes at a library with my parents. By the end of the summer, I knew enough English to enroll as a freshman at Shortridge High School. It became apparent very quickly that I already knew a lot of what the school was trying to teach me; the Realgymnasium I had gone to in Germany was excellent, and I was better prepared than most freshmen at Shortridge. I took a variety of tests and advanced pretty quickly, and at the age of fifteen, I graduated as a senior at Shortridge High School, completing a four-year course of study in only two years.

I was fifteen years old. I had the experience of emigration and the challenge of learning to communicate behind me, but I wasn't especially mature for my age and probably wasn't ready for the working world. My parents were not well-situated, having come so recently from Germany. They could not afford to send me to college. I did get a small scholarship, but it wasn't enough to pay for tuition and expenses. Our relatives said, "Well, he ought to go to work." I got a job at a store called the Star Store in Indianapolis. I worked during the week in the stock room, continuing to improve my English, and on Saturdays, I was a salesman in the men's pant department. This first job was a small primer for all that lay ahead of me. I worked hard to convince my supervisors to let me sell; this minor promotion gave me a first taste of what I could do if I put forth my best effort.

At sixteen, I was able to get a job at Real Silk Hosiery Mills. Real Silk manufactured hosiery and had over 10,000 door-to-door salespeople who sold Real Silk products along with apparel that the company purchased from other manufacturers. Despite the broad retail accessibility of the kind of products Real Silk sold—shoppers could buy hosiery from all manner of retailers—their products were sold exclusively door-to-door. Despite this unusual approach, Real Silk established a strong position in the market rapidly after its founding in 1922. The company had been through rough waters in the 1930s, facing challenges during the Depression and a major labor strike in 1934. As the decade came to an end, the company had recovered some profitability, but it would soon struggle with the same difficulties many manufacturers faced as World War II created supply shortages. My first job there was in manufacturing, as a whizzerboy. A whizzerboy went to work at six in the morning, wetting silk stockings and then drying them in the whizzer—a centrifuge that took the moisture out of the stockings—so that they could be shaped on forms.

After a few months, I got a promotion to become an office boy. Now I didn't have to go to work until eight in the morning. I worked in the sales department, and from there, they had a stock room where customers could come and pick out merchandise. I asked my boss, "Couldn't I work in the stock room helping customers?" He approved. After a while, I realized I liked this selling and asked if I couldn't do more. At this time, I was nineteen or twenty years old. I was allowed to call on customers in town. It was a great opportunity—I didn't know anyone my age, certainly not at Real Silk, who was doing this kind of work.

Though I really liked working and I felt I was growing, I still wanted to go to college. But it just wasn't financially possible; I would have to go about my education through other means. I kept my eyes open at work, looking for new possibilities. I noticed that the company had a lot of rejects and overages and irregulars in its stock. I proposed that we open a retail store in the factory to sell those items to employees. After some consideration, management agreed. Though the company manufactured some war-related materials, consumer-based profits were declining; management was open to new ideas. So I started a retail store in the factory and it went over well. Since it was successful, I suggested that, in addition to selling to employees, we issue five courtesy cards to every employee so their friends or relatives could come in and shop. I organized the courtesy cards, and I had my first business going. We also had plants in Georgia and Mississippi, and I convinced management to open stores in those plants as well. Though I was young and uneducated, it didn't occur to me that the bold suggestions I made were audacious; I saw opportunities. I was obviously restless, and I saw these ideas as beneficial to the company, so that gave me the nerve to go ahead. When I talked to personnel, I was encouraged. So I kept on.

The three retail stores were working: we were getting rid of all of our distressed merchandise. My next step was to go to other companies that had items like this and buy them to sell in our stores. Later, Real Silk gave me the go-ahead to relocate the store so that it had an outside entrance.

At this time, I was 19, still playing with the idea of going to college, but was advised by my relatives that since I'd started to make some money, and college wouldn't make that much difference, it would be best to stick with what I was doing instead of pursuing an education. My parents were getting settled but were not in a position to pay for college. I was continuing to learn many facets of the retail business and had developed abilities that would define my career, but I knew that formal education offered growth that I wasn't experiencing in my work life. So I took night classes at Butler University and at Indiana University Extension in Indianapolis. It was 1944; soon American soldiers would make their way back from the war. Those of us with good jobs would be smart to keep them as men came home looking for work.

I was driven to want to do more and to do better. I continued to pursue more growth within Real Silk, since it was the best avenue available to me. Our retail stores were well-organized; my next step was to go on the road as a salesman. During World War II few people had cars. I took a bus to outlying cities like Crawfordsville, Kokomo, and Muncie. I called on customers to sell them hosiery, and I relished this opportunity, because this was another chance to grow my skills. I now had the experience of being out on the road selling, and having a retail store.

Real Silk maintained its status as a national brand without selling to retail stores. Each month, they had a full-page ad on the back page of *Life* magazine, which was a top publication at the time, so they had very high visibility. On one of my trips, I visited Goldblatt's department store in Chicago. Though I was just selling an odd lot of 150,000 buttons, I asked to see the president. Goldblatt's assumed that Real Silk had decided to pursue a retail presence in their stores and were very excited to see me. Of course, when they learned why I had come, they sent me directly to the button buyer in the basement. But approaching the president of Goldblatt's to sell buttons was an example of the kind of ambition and initiative I carried with me on my sales trips.

I was rapidly outgrowing my position and becoming restless. I began to think it was time to decide what I really wanted to do. The retail business appealed to me. I began to go out to buy products for Real Silk's retail stores—distressed products—and that business kept growing and I thought, "Why can't I go to New York to buy regular products?" I talked management into letting me do it: I got on a bus, went to New York, and looked in the phone book. I had no connections, no access to apparel suppliers. Where could I find people who were selling clothes? I went around, knocked on doors.

By that time I was in my mid-twenties. What I was doing wasn't enough. I was still hungry for more. I had succeeded and had often been able to achieve what I went after and convinced people to let me take new steps. I bought products for Real Silk that sold well, but I kept looking. What else could I do? I decided it was time for me to get into the merchandising end of the business. I wanted to get into the heart of the action. I had so far, despite advancing in position, been on the fringes. I got into merchandising and learned how to pick styles that would have consumer appeal and to write specifications for proper fit and quality. Eventually I thought I was doing a pretty good job and that I might be good at this. Work has always been the laboratory for what I would become. The skills I developed at Real Silk helped me build Paul Harris. I met Earl Harris through a sales relationship. He later became my partner in Paul Harris.

Earl Harris was a dress salesman. Real Silk bought dresses from his company. I went to Chicago about every three months to his company to select certain styles that they would manufacture for us; these would go into our catalogue. This was really a much more interesting business than other occupations I'd had. It gave me a lot of stimulation, a lot of interesting ideas. Real Silk turned the retail stores over to somebody else, since I didn't have time for that any more, and I devoted all my time to developing an outstanding line of products for the catalogue and the door-to-door salespeople. The merchandising skills I was developing were key to the rest of my career. The eye for merchandise that sells can't be taught. I'd had the good fortune to find a way to develop a natural ability. For me, merchandising was always tactile: an ability to approach selections through touch and feel came naturally. The experience I had gained up to this point gave me the confidence to think I had what it took to be very good at this central aspect of the retail business. Though today you'll find retail leaders who emerge from the ranks of finance or operations, historically the stars of the retail industry have been talented merchants.

Earl Harris and I got acquainted; we would often have a drink together in the evening. We had a goal in common: we both would love to have our own business someday. After several months of thinking about it and talking about it, we had the idea of selling apparel in supermarkets. I had been exposed to supermarket retailing in earlier work, and I knew how they did business. Now that I worked in apparel, I thought I would marry those two ideas. It seemed like a modern way to do business. I asked Real Silk whether they would let me sell some of our hosiery in supermarkets if I did it beyond my normal working hours at night and weekends. They said okay because they thought this would be an interesting new concept for their business, and could possibly sell a lot of merchandise.

In 1952 we started a company called Packaged Apparel, and we packaged products in Earl's basement. We talked three different supermarket chains into letting us set up small sections, and suddenly we were in business: Packaged Apparel Incorporated. While today you'll find an assortment of non-grocery products at every supermarket, at the time shopping was much more specialized. An American woman might stop at the market for packaged products and produce, a butcher shop for meats, and a department or discount store for household supplies. Real Silk wasn't interested in maintaining its own retail presence; Packaged Apparel offered that presence, and an unusual and convenient opportunity for women to purchase clothing while making their regular shopping trips. We got up to five different supermarkets. We would haul our packaged products to the stores at night, they would get rung up through the supermarket's cash register, and we would have an accounting once a week. Earl's wife, Carla, kept the books, and we hired two employees to work part time packaging products. We had imagined, and then we had planned. Now we were each working two jobs and had started on our way.

CHAPTER TWO

Paul Harris Takes Root

PACKAGED APPAREL WAS SUCCESSFUL. We were selling a lot of goods, but we realized we were going to be no more than glorified truckers, which wasn't a career for us. We operated much the same way soft drinks are merchandised now: we stocked our products on the shelves and left them unattended until our next visit. We had no control over our merchandise or displays once we left a store.

The people who worked in the supermarkets thought our concept was strange and foreign. We were often placed close to the produce. At one time, we showed up to stock our section only to find a mound of carrots piled on top of our products. Cleaning up carrots wasn't what we'd had in mind. The supermarkets liked it because they could make more mark-up on our apparel than on groceries, but we decided it was not for us. We needed more control of the environment our apparel was displayed and purchased in. The supermarkets had been a good start, but to really grow, we would need the opportunity to develop some kind of relationship with our customer, to be able to specialize to meet her needs. The supermarket sections where Packaged Apparel was displayed severely limited our contact with the people who purchased our offering. We needed a way to get past all these barriers, and eventually we asked: Why don't we open our own retail store? Step by step we closed the apparel sections in supermarkets.

Indianapolis's growth was clustered in suburbs around the city's perimeter. We drove around those suburbs for days, looking for an ideal location to start a retail store. It had to be convenient for women, who did all their family's shopping. It had to be inviting. We found a strip center in Plainfield, southwest of the city. We went to the landlord, who had built the strip shopping center himself. We went to see him to rent a 3,000-square-foot vacant space. Mr. Daum was the landlord. He owned Daum Trucking Company and had decided to build the strip shopping center himself. He said, "Hell, you're nobody, you're not even Three Sisters," which was a chain in those days. We said, "No, you're right, we're not even two sisters, but we'd like to start a store." He obviously didn't have anybody else, so after several weeks of persistence and seven or eight visits, he told us that if we paid in advance, he'd let us have a storeroom. We rented the room, and on December 5, 1954, we opened our first retail store called "Paul Harris" in Plainfield, Indiana. Mr. Daum was quite a doubting Thomas about us; he looked in on us frequently, and after a while, I had the impression he got a kick out of watching us work.

While we were negotiating with Mr. Daum, we went to meet the downtown retailers and asked whether they would consider a branch for themselves in Daum's shopping center. "Hell no," they said. "He wants a dollar a square foot in rent." They thought this was a ridiculous amount of money. Their reactions made us think twice, but we had checked other spots around suburban Indianapolis. They all wanted the same rent, plus a percentage of sales volume. As Daum had built the center himself, his rent was a bit more reasonable. We figured we could do enough sales volume to warrant the expenditure. Further, Plainfield seemed a reasonable middle-class market with residents employed by Public Service Indiana and an encouraging amount of new housing. The supermarket in the center, Standard Grocery Company, was dominant in Indianapolis. We concluded they would bring in plenty of traffic and would be a good neighbor.

I was working during the day in a company that was going nowhere; furthermore, I had occupied enough positions at Real Silk to feel as though I'd learned what I could. I felt that Real Silk had no future, and it seems to me now that starting a retail store was my opportunity to escape. It was ambitious and possibly frightening. It was the biggest risk I'd taken yet. But it was essential that I keep moving forward in my fledgling career. Each time I asked for responsibility and was granted a chance, the wave of momentum at my back swelled. I had known only success. I was ready to take the leap.

We decided that Paul Harris would be the best store in the area, and that we were willing to do things other retailers wouldn't do in order to ensure our success. We took measures that are necessary now, in our age of convenience, but at the time were unheard-of in Plainfield. We had air-conditioning; we stayed open until nine each evening and had free parking. If you wanted to shop in town, you could go to a dry goods retailer to buy apparel downtown. The stores were dark and dingy, and were open 10:00 to 5:00. We were light, airy, and convenient. The existing stores' offering was usually out of date; we carried merchandise that kept up with the times.

I began Paul Harris with Real Silk's knowledge: I had asked for their permission, which they granted. They said, "Look, you have a forty-hour work week, eight to five; as long as you do your work, what you do beyond that is your own business." So when 5:00 came each day, I got off work and drove to Plainfield, and attended to the retail business in the evening and, of course, every weekend. I was busy, busy enough in fact that I had to stop going to school at night. I drew no income, nor did Earl Harris—he kept his job as well— but we gradually developed some credit so that we could build the foundation for a business.

The first Paul Harris store was a 3,000-square-foot family clothing store selling everything from shoelaces to diapers to men's work clothes to women's dresses to millinery, housedresses, and so on. The store was 30 feet wide by 100 feet deep. Each side had pipes supported by steel brackets to hang clothes or wooden shelves to stack merchandise. The floor had steel fixtures with shelves and a few round racks to hang apparel on. We had fixtured our store based on our experience in supermarkets. It was not a soft look, but it was practical. We had met the people who supplied the fixtures for Stop&Shop, and they had helped us. Earl and I were not mechanics, so we had a terrible time assembling the fixtures. I had gotten married in 1954, and my wife, Dorit, moved to Indianapolis. She understood my ambition and was very supportive. During this time she came in to help and was invaluable in getting the store put together. We used our merchandise to soften the look.

Our customers were mostly housewives stopping in before or

after the supermarket. In the evenings, we got some husbands as well. They were nice working-class people, and the sales staff we hired knew a lot of local people, whom they invited in to shop, which was a big help in getting started. We carefully selected local ladies who knew a lot of the townspeople. Our day manager, Harriet White, was quite social and effectively helped select her crew; the night manager, Joanne, had a different group of friends. There was competition between the two, particularly as the day crew had to do the bulk of the stock work and the night crew did more business. We were able to make them both important.

The sales concept was "self-selection," applied from supermarket techniques. Salespeople were available to help, but customers were invited to browse merchandise without being directed by staff. The store was open from 10:00 A.M. to 9:00 P.M. We hired a day manager, and another came in at 4:00 to be our night manager.

The business started out pretty well. We sold a little of everything, but I thought we ought to be more focused. I knew we couldn't do our best selling so many different products, and we should get rid of some items. I had begun to feel that carrying all this variety didn't present a clear image or direction for our company. I wanted an offering that was to the point, less cluttered, and easy to shop. My instincts and experience in merchandising drove me to specialization. Though our offering and environment were much sharper and fresher than other local retailers, if we continued to carry a random assortment, I knew it would be nearly impossible to stick in our customers' minds as a place they *needed* to visit.

When I told Earl my feelings, he disagreed. He said, "We've got a nice little business here. We can make money in shoelaces and diapers." I explained that there wasn't much margin in shoelaces and diapers, and we could use that space to expand the women's wear, which was more fun, more exciting, and more profitable. We disagreed with one another, and it helped drive me on. This was the beginning of a pattern of negotiation and persistence that would continue until Earl's retirement in the eighties: I pushed for growth and change, he resisted. It forced me to learn, over the years, to understand and articulate my vision more effectively. His resistance was a powerful learning tool.

America's post-World War II culture was optimistic and its economy booming. *Brown v. Board of Education* in 1954 launched the civil rights movement, but those events would take years to impact shoppers in Indianapolis suburbs. Women had left behind their wartime jobs and resumed lives of homemaking and childrearing. That lifestyle was idealized by shows like *Leave It to Beaver* as television took over as America's primary entertainment. The first televised Miss America pageant was broadcast just a few months before we opened our store. The Cold War was gaining momentum, helping what was seen as the American way of life increasingly become a source of pride. Central to this ideal was the efficient, collected, fashionable housewife. As time passed, I kept cutting out products and expanding on the women's clothing lines, which I found were able to fulfill my need for creative work much more effectively than the assorted other products. The notions went, and the millinery, and each time something went something else took its place. We focused more on key categories for women. As we focused, we aimed our sights on that housewife. The increasing importance of fashion in her life helped us grow.

Over a period of months, the business gradually began to change. The more it evolved, the more pleased I was, and the more confident I grew in our future. Through nine months of this, still working our full-time jobs, a storeroom two doors down remained empty. I thought we should expand and get that room. Earl said, "Oh, you've got to be crazy. Furthermore, it's two doors down." But in between that space and ours was a furniture store. If we could talk him into moving, we could break through the wall and double the size of our store. We could have a real business going.

We went to the landlord. He looked at us and said, "How can you do that?" But he had begun to admire the job we were doing, and he was no longer very difficult to convince. We talked the furniture store into moving, and we said we'd move all of their merchandise, and we did. It didn't take any fixturing. We got somebody to break through the wall for a door. So now we had a 6,000-square-foot emporium, and I thought that was great. We had lots more dresses and ladies' sportswear.

I never wanted a little store. I wanted a big store. I wanted a lot of big stores. Earl's vision was not the same as mine. He was more interested in making money. He didn't want me to damage our business by taking extravagant risks. I was adamant that expanding was the thing to do, and I really think, in my own subtle way, I overpowered him with my determination. It was in my nature to take risks, and Earl went along with it.

When it was time to open a second store, I don't think Earl was as opposed as he'd been to our initial expansion. The owners of the chain of Stop&Shop, where Packaged Apparel had once had a department, really liked the principles of our business. They were local people. They were building a new supermarket on Lafayette Road, on the west side of Indianapolis, with two extra storerooms. They wanted one drug store and something else, so we talked to them about renting that room between the supermarket and the drug store. They said, "Well, you boys seem to be okay, you seem to be ambitious." They rented us the space, and we started a second clothing store between a supermarket and a drug store. It was the perfect location: The supermarket drove the traffic, and from the same parking lot, it was easy for customers to look into our store. The new store had a big back room, so we had a little space for an office and a stockroom. That became Paul Harris's first headquarters.

I was mentally ready to enter the business full-time. I had been thinking about it and planning it for quite some time. When I resigned at Real Silk and got ready to devote myself to Paul Harris full-time, I wasn't anxious about the risk. I felt an inner relief, a sense of this being right. Splitting my efforts had been a strenuous chore, and now I was liberated from it. But loyalty is important, so I provided Real Silk with help when they asked, consulting with them several times. I was excited to not have to divide my attention any longer and to tackle the challenges of building a business full-time.

I drew a very modest salary. I was recently married, and we were expecting our first child, so I had ample challenges to drive me toward success. I suspect my parents were nervous about the move. My in-laws weren't happy that their only daughter had moved from New York to Indiana and proposed that they could get me a great job in New York. But I was young and driven and ready to pursue my own dream. So I entered a new chapter in my life and was filled with excitement and eagerness to build a meaningful business and career. I was putting in very long hours, and I was blessed that my wife, Dorit, was fully supportive of the business and my commitment to it. Earl, on the other hand, had lots of children, and his wife always wanted more of his time. Paul Harris was always an enormous part of our family, and Dorit has been supportive of me all my life.

It takes something more than commitment to invite your business into every area of your life and be happy about it. My drive for success was central to who I was, within and outside the company. Would Paul Harris have been successful if I hadn't been motivated to my core to work hard? It's impossible to say; I've never known any other kind of life.

CHAPTER THREE

Locations, Locations, Locations

I WAS WORKING AT PAUL HARRIS all the time. It was my life. I moved into a small office in our second store and hired an employee to help with the paperwork. Earl Harris kept his salesman job and worked at Paul Harris in the evenings and on weekends. We had a small warehouse area in the back of the store, and we serviced the Plainfield store from there. I began to organize the business and concentrate on broadening our base, bringing in more merchandise lines and diversifying our offering.

It was 1956; fashion continued to gain prominence in American women's lives as their social and public roles became more established. That year, the Methodist Church decided to allow women to minister, a significant public change. We were well on our way to the golden age of the Barbie doll, which was introduced in 1959 and helped establish fashion as a priority for young girls, to identify it as an eagerly anticipated feature of adulthood.

Our second location, on Lafayette Road, turned out to be successful. There were no other clothing stores anywhere close by. The real estate area that surrounded the store was flourishing, and the supermarket anchoring the strip center drew a lot of traffic, so the business was doing quite well.

At that time, location was even more important for a retailer than it is today. Now, retailers have many resources to supplement the draw of geography; shops in tucked-away corners of tourist towns might ship products to shoppers all over the world through their websites and have better opportunities to spread the word through mass media, helping customers come to them. But when we expanded, cost prohibited companies our size from disseminating information so broadly. There was no Internet. Our storefronts and word of mouth would have to reel women in. Our choices for store locations were a big reason our first stores launched a successful business. Convenience was an important factor for the women who shopped in our stores.

From that Lafayette Road office and warehouse, we would eventually serve stores all around the city and state. All our profits were devoted to the company's growth and improvement. When business owners begin to succeed, they always have a choice: they can take the money and run or reinvest in the business. We chose to reinvest everything.

Until we expanded, our small retail company had provided few disappointments—I was, on the whole, able to feel satisfied in proportion to the energy I expended. Though nearly all of my life was devoted to Paul Harris—I eventually became known for saying "The company is me"—the rewards were continuous and fulfilling. Expansion would complicate things, bring greater thrills and disappointments. It would also begin to introduce Paul Harris as a household name to the suburban Indiana housewife, who would be our core customer for many years.

With the Lafayette Road location, we were entrenched on the west side of Indianapolis. But not everyone was happy. There were many establishments in the Speedway area, to the south, that were not pleased to have the competition from us. They had been doing business for a certain number of years and felt an entitlement to the area's apparel customer. They thought of us as upstarts and thought that anything they could do to prevent us from building a customer base was fair.

The department stores did most of the apparel business. There were three major department stores in the city, and consumers shopped them frequently. But a few specialty stores thrived in the suburbs. On the west side of Indianapolis, in Speedway (home of the Indianapolis Motor Speedway and the Indy 500) one retailer named Dorothy's did a lot of business with branded apparel lines. Until we arrived they had been immune to competition; our arrival caused them to fight us and hopefully keep the brand-name shoppers to themselves.

So what do you do when you find yourself in a hostile business environment? You try to serve your customer better than the competition. We worked to do a good job, selling the merchandise that customers wanted, providing better service than other stores, and finding new ways to set ourselves apart.

This was my first real experience with competition. Other retailers wanted to strangle us, to keep us from succeeding. I had to devise a plan to keep us moving in the right direction. Our strategy was to keep doing a good job selling quality merchandise and to ingratiate ourselves with our suppliers' salesmen, who controlled the territory, and to their management. In the suburbs, we went after the market for national brands of casual apparel, both to create legitimacy for ourselves and because they were popular with our customers. An example of the process of building relationships with suppliers at that time was with the brand Bobbie Brooks, a leading and recognized name. Their headquarters was in Cleveland, Ohio, and I ventured there to meet their energetic president, Maurie Saltsman. After a return visit or two I was able to build a rapport with him and convince him that we would and could grow. He too was self-made; he had grown up as an orphan. I invited him and his sales manager to come to Indianapolis to see our stores and had them to our house for dinner.

Subsequently we developed a program where our stores reported sales of Bobbie Brooks products daily, which interested them, and they automatically replenished what we had sold. This led to an increase in sales of their products, which made everyone happy. It also helped to hone a strategy that I would continue to employ no matter what business I did. Personal relationships with key partners, particularly vendors, have always turned out to be beneficial, even when I could not plan the ways the relationships would pay off. The key to success in retailing, and in business in general, is having people on your side.

I quickly became restless, and we began to consider our next steps. Contemporary retailers have a wealth of tools at their disposal, from national databanks of shoppers' buying patterns to complicated algorithms for predicting consumer behavior. A retailer considering a new site might evaluate location-specific demographics such as household income, race, age, and gender; they might consider what else has succeeded in a particular neighborhood. Crate and Barrel built a new full-size store at Indianapolis's Fashion Mall in 2006. The *Indianapolis Star* reported that Crate and Barrel's decision was heavily influenced by the successful opening of Saks Fifth Avenue the previous fall in the same mall; Tiffany's has opened a store there since, reporting a similar evaluation. Crate and Barrel and Tiffany's have the information resources to understand that a community where Saks can succeed is a community where they can succeed, too.

In the late 1950s, Paul Harris had none of these resources. We made educated guesses at best. We knew we had established ourselves in two parts of the Indianapolis metropolitan area and that Indianapolis women seemed to like our clothing and stores. The city's growth was still concentrated in the suburbs, and we weren't yet making our offering available to women in many of those suburbs. Getting a foothold on each side of town seemed like a natural way to grow. We decided to surround Indianapolis with Paul Harris stores in locations like the Lafayette Road strip center. This would turn out to suit the city's growth, as well; the majority of its top retail areas developed along and still lie in a ring around the periphery, marked on today's maps by the I-465 interstate bypass. We opened a store in Nora Plaza on the north side, Devington Plaza on the east side, Twin Air on the southeast, and so on. These stores were all strip shopping centers, and they were quite successful. Staying in outlying neighborhoods helped us continue to be conveniently located for the city's homemakers.

After this expansion, Paul Harris had eight stores, and it was apparent that we needed to develop some people to help run the organization. I always wanted people to succeed and always had a lot of faith that people could do a good job. I felt that if people wanted to do more, they should have that opportunity. I had come up through Real Silk and grown my own company driven by this kind of thinking, and I always assumed others would benefit from that attitude. The many successful employees who would grow up in the company to achieve high goals are my best achievements in business, the accomplishment of which I'm most proud.

Clearly this faith in people described the way I conducted myself. In every company I had worked for and in the company I now owned I always looked for opportunities to expand my abilities and take on more responsibility. The aptitudes I hoped our employees could develop in merchandising and business were difficult or impossible to teach. How, then, would I go about training someone else?

Merchandising is the heart of the retail business. No matter what else you offer—convenience, great salespeople, smart advertising—the only part of your company a customer takes home is the products you sell. The only way to get shoppers to come back is to offer the quality and style of merchandise they need. I was beginning to hone our offering into a selection that would be focused and specialized. I realized that I wouldn't be able to keep doing all the buying as we grew. I had made the acquaintance of Walter Salmon, a leading professor of retailing at Harvard University, and visited him to learn more about how to grow people. He had a theory he called "Green Thumb," meaning that to be a successful retail merchant one needed to have a green thumb. As a gardener has a sensitivity for plants, a merchant needs a sensitivity for merchandise. While many other skills could be taught, the green thumb was a trait a merchant naturally had or lacked.

Hoping to fill the gap, we granted our office clerk a promotion to become a buyer. I had high hopes. As a buyer, her intentions were good, but she just didn't have the knack for it. After that experience, I decided it was time to hire a professional buyer, someone who had cut teeth at another firm and would bring practiced skills to our young staff. After a search around the city, I found a woman in a downtown store who was looking for a change. So I hired our first professional buyer.

I told her the position would be very time-consuming. I assumed that the position she had at her previous job was time-consuming as well. She said the hours would not be a problem, and I believed that she would be willing to do the job no matter how long it took. I was wrong. After a few weeks, she began to be disturbed by the hours and was not prepared to work the kind of schedule I kept. She believed that I was in the fast lane to the cemetery, and she wanted to enjoy her life.

I maintained my belief in people's ambition and drive throughout my career. But as our growing business required more and more personnel, I found repeatedly that people would talk a good game, but when it got down to it, they really didn't want to succeed as much as I did. I didn't see my commitment as a sacrifice; I did what was necessary to do a good job. But not everyone shared my views. We kept bringing in other people. It was a slow process to find young people who wanted to devote whatever it takes to success. I wasn't on a fast track to the grave; I was thriving, because this wasn't work to me in any negative sense. I loved what I did. I would have to find people who shared that trait, not just those who were skilled. This was a problem that we faced over and over again as we built the company.

Soon Earl Harris left his sales job and joined the business full-time, and we began to divide our duties. He took charge of real estate, and he dealt with the various strip center developers to secure locations, and he also supervised the employees in the stores. My job was to merchandise, do all the buying, plan what we were going to have to sell, and to oversee the internal operations. We discussed what we each felt we would be good at. I had always had my eye on the merchandise. He was a salesman with a tough exterior, which would be useful for negotiating leases.

The business continued to grow, and the decisions became more complex. As I looked at the successful retailers, I saw that they managed their affairs with the help of a computer.

Computers were new and incredibly expensive; they were only used at that time by much larger companies than ours. With more stores, there were more complications, and I decided to look for a way to manage all the complex information. At the time, if you could not afford these large and expensive computers, you could rent the use of computers from other companies.

We made a deal with Remington Rand, a service bureau, to rent time on a computer service they had, so that we could begin to have some meaningful records that would help us plan how much to buy, what to mark down, when to mark it down, and begin to orchestrate a businesslike approach to what we were doing. The Remington Rand computer system worked on punch cards; we delivered the cards to their service bureau and they printed a report each weekend, after Saturday's business was in. We would evaluate them every Monday. This systematized our business and worked out fine for two years.

Though we faced challenges, these were exciting years. The early years of Paul Harris had lots of growing pains, lots of disappointments, but also lots of success: we did keep growing. We attracted a group of young people who wanted to be a part of our exciting organization, and business was getting to be more competitive. By this time, we had become a factor in suburban Indianapolis retailing for women and were beginning to have some recognition in the marketplace.

We had also continued to change our product mix, and change was always the order of the day. We continued to revisit our corporate philosophy and used this philosophy to update our offering. We did away with most menswear and expanded the womenswear part of the business, which was quicker, more exciting, and changed more often. I felt it held a much greater opportunity than menswear, since the vast majority of our shoppers were women. We kept a table or rack of some men's apparel in each store, but it was geared for either the wives to buy something for their husbands if they had a guilty conscience about buying for themselves, or for men who shopped with their wives. But the menswear was a defensive type of offering, rather than the aggressive play of becoming more specialized in womenswear. We carried womenswear for the suburban housewife and were sportswear-oriented. We had lines like Jantzen, Catalina, and White Stag; shorts, slacks, tops, and t-shirts. These were recognized national brands and made up the thrust of our business.

In order to build the types of business relationships that I think are important, for each line, I made it a point to travel to the headquarters of the company to meet management, just as I had done with Bobbie Brooks. It became important to them and it helped us to get an edge from them at the end of the season, when they cleared their stocks out at 30 percent off regular prices.

Our established merchandising and computerized recordkeeping helped us to recognize a need to turn our stocks more quickly and get rid of things at the end of each season. Women's apparel is an almost entirely seasonal business. Every dollar's worth of merchandise that didn't sell took up a dollar I couldn't spend on the next season's offering. In order to get cash from merchandise that had not sold I developed the idea of a semi-annual sale. While this might seem commonplace in 2007, at the time the semi-annual sale was unusual. It was designed to clear out merchandise and generate a predictable influx of cash twice a year.

In preparation for our semi-annual sale we would close each store for half a day while we marked all the merchandise down, and we sent postcards to all of our customers to let them know the big semi-annual sale was on. This really turned people on, and it changed our business and our work lives considerably. By eight A.M. on sale days, we had lines in front of our stores. People would buy merchandise by the armload and felt good about it because we had deep markdowns on proven merchandise they had seen before.

This continued to grow into an established event that got to be known city-wide. Eventually, we were sending postcards to a large number of people. If we were going to have a sale starting on a Tuesday or Wednesday, people would come into the store a day or two before, line up what they wanted to buy, and hide it behind a mirror so that they could come the moment the store opened and pick their selections up. We had tremendous crowds—you couldn't walk through the store during our sales. We had dressing rooms, but they didn't accommodate the crowds. People would go to change in the back room. Some people would try things on right in the aisles. It was wild. We had long lines at the registers.

On sale days, we would do thousands of dollars of business in the first few hours, and it would keep going all day and for the next few days. We cleaned out our stock quickly, created a lot of cash, and then, after a week, brought in our next season's merchandise. We also learned to go to our suppliers and ask them to sell us their remaining products at the end of the season at a third off or so, and we could in turn put those items on sale. We had a lot to sell. Upon examination, we learned that the sales amounted to 30 to 35 percent of our season's business.

Paul Harris's semi-annual sales got to be known as the best sale in town, but there were drawbacks. Our customers weren't luxury shoppers; we geared our offering to homemakers who were interested in good quality at a good price. People developed an inclination to wait for the sales rather than buying when merchandise was new. It seemed dangerous to continue to be geared so heavily to sales. We risked getting a reputation that all we were good for was a sale, which would cause a certain decline in full-price purchases.

The semi-annual sales had combined with our growing momentum to help our stores around Indianapolis become successful.

We decided it was time to go statewide in order to continue our momentum and expand. We opened stores in Richmond, Crawfordsville, Kokomo, Bloomington, and so on. We used toned-down but similar tactics for our statewide sales. To address the problem of setting up sales out of the city, I began to organize working teams of six to seven people—either managers from other stores or headquarters staff we had started to develop. We would go on a Sunday to a certain city, and when the store closed, we would revamp the whole store to get set for the sale Monday morning. The teams would have to stay over because we worked until ten or so at night to get the sale set up and mark all the merchandise down, to be ready for the onslaught that would come Monday morning.

Our substantial time commitment to the sales caused a bit of a problem in the running of the company. We'd work ourselves so hard that we couldn't attend to some of the other things we needed to do, and we were so often away. The demands on our time and energy exemplified the pace of Paul Harris's growth. The same demands would continue to present challenges in growing our staff, but it also helped ensure that those who stayed on were up for great challenges.

I made the decision to gradually find a way to lower the impact of our sales. Of course, customers wouldn't like it. But we had no choice: we had to succeed in lessening the impact of our sales without alienating our customer base. We worked endless hours, and it got to the point where we would have a sale at the east side store but not the west, for example, and people would travel to the different parts of the city, because we couldn't handle sales at all the stores on the same day. Toning down the sales caused us to lose quite a bit of business, but we increased the profit on the things we did sell.

This was a time in my career when I learned that evolution has to be manageable. The necessity of building an organization while pushing the business forward had never been so evident; we would have to change in ways we understood and ways we could keep in control.

It was 1959, and by that time, we had nineteen stores. We had been in business for five years, had developed good contacts with our manufacturers, and had structured an organization. We had processes in place. We had customers who appeared to be well-served by Paul Harris.

We also had many good employees. They were bright and motivated. They did their jobs well. My job as a leader of a company was to find people and develop them into the stars of the business. Two problems always emerged with this. Either employees could not sustain their excellence or they left for better offers. I remember one young man who showed great promise. He was a buyer and did very well, and I hoped he could become my successor in merchandising. He was married, had two kids, and his wife wanted more of his time. She objected to the kind of hours he was putting in, particularly on the weekends. He was really conflicted: he liked what we were doing, but his wife was unhappy. I sensed the problem; we would talk about it. I kept thinking it would get resolved over a period of time. After a couple of years, he came to me and said he really liked our business, he liked what he was doing, but his wife didn't want him to continue, so he either had to get to a point where he could work a forty-hour week or he'd have to quit. He knew that a forty-hour week would never be possible, and he left the company.

Something else was happening at this time in the retail environment. Malls were beginning to appear. Paul Harris stores were only in strip shopping centers, both in Indianapolis and around the state. I began to think that the future of retailing would take place in the malls, that the place for us to grow was in malls. Earl and I didn't agree. He felt we had a good business going. We were enjoying it, we were successful, we were doing very well in the family-oriented stores that we had. If we went into malls, where there were big department stores and specialty stores, he feared we wouldn't fit. It was a different kind of business; we wouldn't stand out as much as we did in the neighborhood strips. I felt for us to grow and become a factor, we had to get into malls, and not just stay in strip shopping centers. Earl was right; it *was* a different kind of business. Our next milestone of change was upon us.

CHAPTER FOUR

Paul Harris Goes to the Mall

AMERICA'S FIRST FULLY-ENCLOSED SHOPPING MALL opened in Edina, Minnesota in 1956. It was designed by a Viennese architect who had emigrated in 1938, the same year my family came to America. The idea behind the mall was to take all the best elements of a city's downtown retail area and enclose them in a tightly controlled environment. As urban residents were becoming more affluent and escaping the problems of the city by moving to the suburbs, downtown retailers were losing customers. Malls anticipated this demographic shift by building along those highways being built to support the suburban migration of customers.

In malls, smaller retailers were able to benefit from the heavy advertising and broad selection of huge department store anchors, which would get shoppers in the door. Developers could control everything from the lighting to the texture of the floor beneath a woman's shoes, optimizing the shopping experience and enhancing the buying mood. Some of the most successful developers rent stores strategically so that neighboring retailers benefit from like-minded shoppers, while every area benefits from consumers vacillating between giant retail anchors.

The opening of the first enclosed shopping mall attracted journalists from all the major publications; it inspired reports that the mall had instantaneously become central to American culture. Of course, we recognize, nearly 50 years later, the accuracy of these claims. The shopping mall is the icon of American consumerism. It changed not only the entire retail industry, but the actual shape of American cities, driving consumer traffic out of downtowns toward

33

enormous suburban megaplexes. Mall developers took advantage of the evolving interstate highway system. The interstates, built in the mid- to late fifties and originally designed to drive urban renewal, had facilitated the opposite: people could now live farther than ever from the places they worked. As families settled outside urban areas and men commuted to work, convenient retail areas like the ones where Paul Harris stores were located paved the way for mall development. Malls sprang up along interstate highways on the outskirts of midwestern cities. Today more than half of all retail shopping happens in an enclosed shopping mall.

By the time I convinced everyone at Paul Harris to give mall retailing a try in 1969, it was obvious that the mall was America's retail future. If we were going to continue on our path of growth and success, that's where we should build our new stores. Our conversations and disagreements forced me to sharpen my reasoning, to consider the possible consequences of this kind of risk in great detail. We were doing very well in our current locations. Success is difficult to argue with. And it was true, we didn't know all the risks involved, didn't know what moving our business into malls would require of us. We had built a nucleus of an organization, and we discussed the options with our employees. Their opinions were split, and they looked to Earl and me for leadership. Gradually, I won out: we would add one mall store to our roster and see how it went.

We opened our first mall store in Dayton, Ohio, with our usual merchandise mix, which was a variety of apparel for housewives and for younger women. Locating our first mall store in Ohio rather than Indiana was a matter of timing and circumstance: a new mall was being built at the time that looked like a great place to start. We hadn't developed our merchandise offering into any specific kind of niche or focus, which worked out fine in strip centers; housewives and younger women stopped in after grocery shopping or made a trip out to pick up apparel. We weren't situated in direct proximity to our competition in strip centers. But in a mall we learned very quickly that this same strategy would not work. The one or two anchor stores in the mall carried the same types of things we carried. The other successful mall stores were specialty retailers with extremely focused offerings for either young women, housewives, or plus sizes. Our a-little-of-this-and-that merchandise mix didn't attract mall shoppers. Our fixturing, too, was off the mark, geared toward our usual strip center customers. Our friendly, unsophisticated store design was fine if you were coming in anyway, but it wouldn't attract anyone visually from the outside. The store was bland, the offering was all over the map, and it appeared that we had a disaster on our hands.

The strongest retailers in the mall at that time were The Limited, Casual Corner, Lerner's, Ups and Downs, Merry Go Round, Three Sisters, and Gap. The Limited was the hot store at the time. I was envious of what they were doing and felt they were more creative than many other retailers. It seemed that the successful mall stores were specialized to an extreme. The Limited, for example, would pin down one sweater they knew would sell well—presumably, they had tested it beforehand—and focus all their energy on it. They would feature it in all the available colors on a table at the store's entrance. They would successfully saturate the market with that one key item. I wanted to know, how could they hone in on one thing, and do it so well? We were struggling because we weren't yet specialized enough; the mall's star was succeeding by specializing to the point of focusing on one singular thing.

Paul Harris strip stores were still doing well, but the mall store was losing money. We were a bit of a laughingstock in the eyes of mall shoppers. One thought within the organization was that we should admit that we didn't belong in that kind of marketplace and close the store. But I was certain that malls were the future of the retail apparel business; if we were to continue to grow, we would have to become sophisticated and successful in malls. I also didn't want to admit defeat. It wasn't in my nature to give up. We spent at least a half a year struggling, experimenting with specialization of merchandise, and finally settled on apparel for young women.

Along with this new merchandise focus, every aspect of the mall store had to change. To start with, we had to improve the look and feel of the mall store. The Limited's displays were enticing. I loved the way they presented their offering, with items hung together as a complete look in a provocative, sexy way. We hired an extremely creative young man to develop our mall displays; he did wonderful display work. He flew dresses and merchandise from ceilings and walls. This dramatic new look was designed to attract the attention of young, vibrant women to our store. Inside, they found carefully merchandised sportswear and apparel, prom dresses in the spring, and an entirely redesigned offering. If we could continue to find new ways to bring women into our stores and offer consistently appealing merchandise, we might be fine. We had evolved from being a general women's apparel store into a highly specialized young women's apparel store with a recognizable look, stylish decor, and a creative atmosphere. We had found the way to stand out in the malls as effectively as we did in strip centers. Our store looked exciting. The look and the merchandise seemed to gel together. People came in and were interested in what we were doing.

The evolution toward mall success required changing the architecture of the mall store. We hired a different kind of architect to give the structure itself a unique look. The local architect we used for our strip centers designed stores primarily for customers' comfort and convenience; his work wouldn't maximize our visibility in malls. I researched and interviewed quite a few store architects and had them visit our store to critique it. Two highly creative architects from a California firm convinced me that they could put together an attention-getting store with wooden beams and unusual fixtures. The wooden beams as part of the design were unusual; they created a unique space to display and sell jewelry around the register area. They also developed fun and colorful graphics for the wall area, using strong colors. I hired them to develop our next mall store, which was opening in Cincinnati. Again, the choice of location was based largely on timing and circumstance. The store was expensive to build and their design wasn't entirely functional, so we had to make adjustments. But it was unique. Our Cincinnati store gave us a fresh start in mall retailing.

Once we figured out the mall store's two primary challenges—attracting shoppers visually and offering specialized items—we had to turn our attention to ongoing struggles. Our semi-annual sale didn't work as well in the mall; people wouldn't line up outside, so we had to have normal sales to clean our merchandise. And for quite some time, I got carried away with our display specialist. He did beautiful, extravagant work and was extremely creative and ambitious, and his enthusiasm got the better of me. We were creating new displays every two weeks, using costly, beautiful fixtures, spending excessive amounts of time and money reworking displays so often. Our mannequins were very different and costly, while other stores were commercial in their display fixtures and approach. We were probably carried away with uniqueness.

He also convinced me to build a display department within our organization, with artists who created vibrant, elaborate posters and display items for our stores. Out of the display ideas, we developed an artistic department, with two women who painted posters and developed visually attractive artwork for our mall stores. We developed an extremely unusual poster with a rainbow and the slogan, "Paul Harris is the Place." We even developed in-store music about our "Place." I became entranced with the creativity and loved the notion of setting ourselves apart so effectively.

I might have gone overboard in my enthusiasm, forgetting to be businesslike, but the whole endeavor satisfied my creative urges. There has to be a healthy balance between creativity and business decisions. First and foremost, one always has to realize that a business requires your full attention. Employees and stockholders depend on your running at least a break-even business, and hopefully making a profit. You can spend hundreds of thousands of dollars and have unique and incredible designs and then find that although it improved sales it did not increase profit. Someone must always keep an eye on the financial ball, and as I got lost in the creativity of what we were doing I risked losing sight of the business.

None of the high-style materials we developed for the mall stores was very effective or useful in our strip center stores; the tactic wasn't suited to those shoppers, and the merchandise there was still a varied and bland offering. At this point, we were spending money, time, and energy developing these looks for only two stores: one in Dayton and one in Cincinnati. But it was beginning to be apparent that we *could* succeed in the mall marketplace. We weren't making money yet, but we were getting noticed. We were making a mark. It looked like we could profit steadily in mall environments, so I convinced the organization to turn our future in that direction; from this point forward, we would open new stores only in malls. We found locations all around Ohio, where malls were developing rapidly, and began to spread out in the Midwest. The large markets, where there was excessive competition, were difficult for us, but in smaller malls, where there were fewer competitors, we had the chance to stand out more and began to have a foothold.

As we grew, I spent much of my time with the display staff, doing exciting work in developing new ideas and furthering the look we'd begun to establish. I'm not sure that changing our displays every two weeks was prudent, but it was an awful lot of fun, and it kept my creativity engaged. The market began to demand that we pay attention to more than just our look. As long as we carried national brands, we were placing ourselves in direct competition with the anchor department stores, whose advertising dollars and enormous presence could always win out. To succeed in the long run, we would have to distinguish our products as well as our displays. We had to develop our own clothing lines.

The creative work of developing a store's look fulfilled me; developing a product line was thrilling beyond my imagination. It would change not only the way we did business, but my whole life. I saw the world merchandising our stores, and learned by trial and error a whole new way of doing business.

CHAPTER FIVE

Breaking New Ground: Designing a Brand

WE HAD NO GUIDE TO RELY UPON as we built our organization. Sometimes you can lean on the expertise of experienced executives to make difficult decisions; sometimes your own experience serves as a road map. Other times you guess and hope you come out right more often than wrong. Though the company was coming together, we still had much to learn. Each time we did something new, we had to accomplish two things: we were implementing a new procedure we would hope to repeat as a consistent process, but we were also building an organization with every step, attending to the thrills and complications of growth.

In building Paul Harris I found that the development and manufacture of our own unique clothing line for each season was unbelievably thrilling. At that time, there weren't a lot of experts waiting in line to guide us through that process. Most often, retailers visited manufacturers' showrooms in New York to shop from lines the manufacturers had developed or contracted a buying office to study their companies and select merchandise they thought would suit the retailers' customers. But we were pioneering another way of retailing. When a retailer purchases a line from a manufacturer, the retailer pays the cost of design and development with the manufacturer's profit added on. When you design and manufacture your own line, you have greater control of the design costs, which leads to increased profits. As a general rule, private branding—designing and branding your own merchandise—is more profitable than buying and selling name-brand merchandise. Name-brand merchandise offers a retailer the advantage of recognizability and a built-in following. Name-brand apparel should also offer the expertise of a proven group of executives who hopefully know more than you do about what the customer will want in colors, styles, and so forth. Name-brand merchandise also provides advertising that doesn't add to the retailer's expenses. So although name-brand merchandise makes a retailer less money on average, it cuts down a retailer's risk.

But I wasn't interested in avoiding risk. The company was my life; all this trailblazing was my vehicle for personal growth. I had never been one to wait for instructions. Like everything else I had done, I would learn this, too, by experience. I couldn't have asked for a better educational opportunity than the development and manufacture of Paul Harris brands. The world travel and cultural exchange that started with creating successful product lines became a way of life for me and my family; throughout my career and since my retirement I've remained devoted to seeing and experiencing the world.

Paul Harris made its first attempts at product development in the United States, but this turned out to be expensive and difficult for a company of our size. U.S. vendors required large minimum purchases and were generally inflexible about making style changes, which directly defeated one purpose of Paul Harris branding. American manufacturing companies were also very expensive. We looked for an alternative and explored the possibility of manufacturing our lines outside the United States. Many American manufacturers were already moving their facilities to other countries to defray some costs. It became apparent that the best way to go about manufacturing our own lines would be to manufacture in Asia.

Today the majority of U.S. apparel is manufactured in other countries. American consumers are simply not willing to pay the prices retailers would have to charge if they sold apparel produced in the United States. But in the early 1970s, international commerce, particularly between American and Asian companies, was much less established and far more complicated than it is today.

As we were developing our first private brand apparel, the Asian factories were just beginning to establish apparel manufacturing dominance. If you'd like to develop products in Asia today, you'd have endless resources available: electronic communication, sophisticated Chinese business agents, proven techniques documented by American companies that led the way. But we started out with nothing but skill and luck.

Early in the 1970s, I made my first trip to Hong Kong and contracted with a small agency to take us around to factories and get us acquainted. The agents weren't especially professional, but they were nice people. It was a husband and wife, and it became apparent to me that they carried little weight or respect with the factories. I brought sketches to be made for us and sold with our own label. So we began in a very amateurish way to make our own products and import them to distinguish ourselves from the department stores.

Our first attempt was mediocre, and I knew we had to get a lot better. We didn't have much of a process in place. One way to improve was to find a more professional agent. I picked up the names of other agents and worked on researching them when I got home. One agent, Li Fung, impressed me. The agency was very personal and was growing rapidly. It had first-class clients, such as the Gap. Today, Li Fung is by far the biggest agent in the Orient. After we had been with the agency for some time, I began to feel that it was so big that the service it rendered became too impersonal for our needs. On subsequent trips to the Orient, I quietly researched to locate another agent. We got together with a smaller, more aggressive agent who was well-suited to our specialized needs. All these negotiations were essential to getting established with the Asian manufacturers, with whom American companies couldn't yet do business directly.

Today, doing business with China seems simple and commonplace. In the 1970s it was very different. In those years, the United States hadn't normalized relations with China, much less begun a national discussion of the ramifications of business relations. There was no way of doing direct business with Chinese companies. Just to get permission to visit, we had to work through tremendous amounts of red tape. I had to call our senator to help us arrange an invitation.

Like so many other components of building the company, we learned to manufacture in the Orient by trial and error. Soon after starting out, we were doing business in Hong Kong, Japan, and Taiwan. China, however, was the most attractive place to manufacture apparel because its prices were much lower than Hong Kong's.

I worked to get an invitation to the Canton Fair, a semi-annual event where all the Chinese manufacturers come together at a trade show. Retailers from all over the world come to the fair to check out the quality and variety of apparel available. But it was not as simple as mailing in an application and paying a registration fee. Since our first trips, the U.S. government has established agencies whose mission is to help increase foreign trade. But we had to make several appeals just to secure our first invitation to the event.

Even after we had a foot in the door, doing business with Chinese manufacturers wasn't so simple. Cultural differences present additional challenges to doing business. The Chinese manufacturers didn't trust new clients. We ordered T-shirts and wanted to talk about the colors. The manufacturer said, "You're not a friend yet. This year, we'll sell you white. Next year, when you're a friend, we'll talk about colors." This obviously wasn't going to work for Paul Harris customers.

And although the Asian companies had great manufacturing, they didn't have any creative or product development people. They were set up strictly for the manufacture of products designed by the buyers. On later trips, we came better prepared. And as we became better "friends," the manufacturers would show us items they were making for other companies, and we would make changes and order merchandise from those copies.

But most often, because we could not depend on the Asian sources for design, we had to show up with our own ideas and samples ready for production. For each season's new line, we took buyers to the boutiques of Europe to develop ideas. I would go with two or three people to Paris, London, and Milan, where we'd buy clothing we thought Paul Harris customers would love. We modified items— a collar from one blouse, a bodice from another—defining our line. We took our purchases to be sketched and sent our sketches to the Asian factories. A month later, we traveled to Asia to check out our samples and negotiate prices and delivery. We were developing a whole new kind of retailing and a new kind of life. Of course, all of this travel and design seems very glamorous; it was a vital part of my growth. But being a good buyer is hard work. We didn't always have leisure time. Work was twelve to fifteen hours per day. It was exciting because it was very creative, and I didn't need to rest or relax; the work itself kept me energized.

This new way of life gave me tremendous pleasure. I loved going to Europe, seeing new things. These were the trips that first sparked my passion for art. I bought the first item in our collection on a merchandising trip to Italy. Throughout our lives, my wife and I have continued to build our eclectic collection and have become deeply involved in the arts.

Traveling, of course, broadened my perspective in countless ways. I saw great buildings, ate wonderful food, and met many interesting people. This was all a big change for me, coming from Indianapolis. I saw new kinds of retailing, too. I made contacts at Selfridge's, a big department store in London, to get their best-selling items so that we could adapt them. Europe was always six months to a year more advanced in fashion ideas than the United States, so we were able to use their lines to help anticipate our customers' desires.

Over time, we expanded our manufacturing locations. Each new manufacturer in a new country was an exciting growth experience. A great deal of the fun for me, as well, was having two or three people whom we were developing at home to make these trips with me, seeing them grow as people and as professionals. We were devoted to the work. We would have arguments in Hong Kong: what to make, what not to make, how much to pay, when to have it shipped. Bringing them up in the company and inviting them to challenge my ideas with their own was an integral part of the trips. Of course, we never forgot what we were there for: to bring exciting products to the women of the American Midwest at prices that they could afford.

We faced challenges at each step. We had to learn to negotiate deliveries, terms, quality control, getting samples, and timing, all with the help of our Asian agents. We had culture shocks, too. In China, for example, a typical group meal is served by placing many dishes in the center of a table, often on a spinning device like an enormous lazy susan, and inviting everyone to share dishes, picking from the many family-style plates with their chopsticks as the selections rotate around the table. We were often served lunches in the factories, with a meal in this style laid out on a work table. We had a buyer who couldn't eat this way. We had to cross all the cultural boundaries with the usual care and attention, too, to avoid getting sick from eating and drinking the wrong things. Everything was new.

When we started doing business overseas the Asian businesspeople were as culturally unsophisticated as we were. One blouse we brought from Europe as a sample had a cigarette burn one of our buyers had accidentally left in the pocket. We didn't think much about it, assuming the manufacturers would recognize it as accidental damage. But the manufacturer believed that they were to copy the design exactly as we'd given it to them. When our shipment arrived, all the pockets had cigarette burns.

Fit and quality were also problems with manufacturing in the Orient early on. There were really no apparel standards for sizing. One manufacturer's small is another's medium. One's size 12 is another's 10. To minimize sizing errors, we had to hire a person to be in charge of our quality control. He visited the factories overseas to check the production and make sure we would get the quality and fit we required for our stores. Another task was color control; integral to our brand was a unique color offering each season, and we had to take steps to be sure the garments would all match and work together. This was a time-consuming but essential part of our product development work.

Over time, Asian manufacturers and agents became more sophisticated about American business and cultural practices. Situations like the burned pockets happened less and less. People from all over had begun manufacturing there, and the more experienced companies in Hong Kong became more professional—and also more expensive. As Asian manufacturing evolved, we broadened our reach, working in Malaysia and India. Some of those countries were very inexpensive because they were in the very earliest stages of this new international commerce. In India, we would be in factories to work on samples, and a power failure would halt everything. We might sit in a hot, dark room sweating for half an hour, hoping for the power to come back on. The whole city of New Delhi had these electricity shortages on a daily basis.

At one point, we decided to expand our manufacturing in India. They had attractive colorations and fabrics that we knew our consumers would appreciate. On our first trip to India, my agent said we should go to the south of India, to Madras, because they had the most unusual fabrics and colors. We wanted to work there, not only in New Delhi. So naturally, two of our buyers and I decided to go, and the day we left New Delhi, I wasn't feeling very well. Of course you have to be careful what you eat, and I thought I had been very careful. But on the plane to Madras, I got awfully sick. By the time we landed, I had a hard time even getting off the plane. We got to the hotel, and I was just as sick as I could be. I was up all night, not sleeping. I knew I was in Madras to work, so I got up in the morning. We were picked up to go to a textile manufacturer to choose fabrics.

As miserable as I felt, I went along because I said, "How can I justify being here and staying in sick?" I got to the factory, and I couldn't use their bathroom, because it was a hole in the floor. We had a car that took me to a place close by. Back in the factory, I was working with our buyer, and all of a sudden things just went blank and I passed out. So they took me back to the hotel. I couldn't keep any food or drink down. After another day of just having tea, I was able to get back to work. That was one of the more frightening experiences. There were many more like that in various parts of the world. When I look back upon it, it was interesting and exciting, although obviously it wasn't all pure fun. These experiences were all part of an important growth pattern. I would expect that as U.S. retailers have made themselves part of the business landscape in India, Malaysia, the Philippines and all the other countries we manufactured in, there has been a marked improvement in utilities, sanitation, hotel and dining accommodations, and infrastructure. I can only hope that the outsourcing of manufacturing has led to an improvement in the quality of life for the people of those cities and communities.

We, too, were becoming more sophisticated at product development and Asian manufacture. We used unusual fabrics and made shirts and blouses. In India, it was very hard to do pants—they didn't have zippers. People in the United States didn't want just buttons. So we went through a whole period of growing and learning about how to make products overseas and how to build an organization structured around successful day-to-day operation at home, and extensive travel for our buyers and me. We established relationships in London and Paris, too, to make getting samples more effective and systematic. Selfridge's, in London, provided me with extensive information to help make decisions. Since Europe's fashion sense was so far ahead of America's, I thought it would be a great idea to shop Selfridge's juniors department and find out what I could about the sales of items that interested me. We developed a system where I would find an item I was considering, and they would provide me with a printout of sales figures for that item. In theory, this should have made our lines more successful, but I can't think of a single example of a product for which this system produced results. We had a similar arrangement with Au Printemps in Paris; this too, didn't seem to produce the results we'd expected.

Up until this point in the business, the design, development, and manufacture of apparel was my territory. I loved it. It was creative. Merchandising was then and still is the heart of retailing. But as you take on more responsibility in a company, you sometimes lose those things that bring you the most joy, fulfillment, and challenge. I had to begin to share the buying responsibilities. Although I wanted to lead our product development, I also recognized that in time, we needed people who could take this over entirely, and we would need to develop some kind of oversight of quality; we had our agents, but they sometimes weren't careful enough and approved things for shipment that did not meet our standards. These products didn't always fit right, and then we had big problems and needed compensation. This led to a need for a program to sell these things at a discount. This was a real period of learning, but it was exciting, and it seemed like every week brought us a new challenge. We were learning how to make our own line, how to develop our own products, how to be different from everybody else, and at the same time, build an organization. Once in Hong Kong, we had two buyers who didn't see eye to eye, and at one point, it got so bad that in the conference room in our agent's working area, the two buyers actually got into a fistfight. I had to pull them apart. But conflict and challenge were part of doing business.

By the mid- to late seventies, we had established a systematic, effective merchandising strategy built around seasonal travel for idea development, manufacturing, and quality control. Our lines had become consistently appealing and innovative, with a series of hallmarks that guided our buyers. We made branding and merchandising look easy. But to get this far, we had to overcome daily doubts and difficulties, cultural barriers, and dozens of mishaps, mistakes, and miscommunications. We succeeded because we were persistent and eager to try something new at each obstacle, but even more because the challenges were part of what we loved. The merchandising trips had redefined my life. I could no longer imagine marking the passing of a season while staying in one place, doing the same thing week after week. We went from breaking new business ground to systematizing product development and Asian manufacturing in a span of only a few years, and along with a few other retailers, we paved the path that most apparel retailers follow today.

CHAPTER SIX

All Around the World

YOU HAVE HEARD THE EXPRESSION "It's lonely at the top." Managers speak to other managers. Sales associates speak to other associates. Buyers speak to other buyers. But often there isn't anyone in a company that CEOs can be completely open with. During the years when Paul Harris was developing its own lines I joined the Young Presidents' Organization. YPO was one of the many opportunities my position offered me; like the other doors Paul Harris opened, I saw it as a chance to grow as a person and to help the company.

The Young Presidents' Organization is made up of people who are presidents of their companies and whose companies have five million dollars or more in annual volume and employ at least 100 people. You must qualify by the time you are 40 years old, and you are expelled at the age of 50, at which point you get a rocking chair.

YPO is a great learning organization. It has two annual "universities," where many famous businesspeople come and give courses; YPO also sponsors various learning seminars and has monthly chapter meetings. The organization is still thriving today. Over the years, YPO offered me excellent opportunities to make connections with other retail companies, to travel, and to represent Paul Harris to businesspeople across America and around the world. The YPO and other similar organizations provide a level of support for people in those stressful positions and provide enrichment opportunities that help them run their organizations. Staying educated was an important part of my mission, both personally and professionally. I had already made a habit of establishing a rapport with suppliers and other business associates. YPO would help me make connections for our future and give me the chance to see how retailers worked around the country and around the world.

Early on, the group asked me to chair a seminar on retailing. It was a traveling seminar, with about forty presidents at retailing companies or stores that sold to retailers. We went to Edison Brothers in St. Louis, Dayton Hudson in Minneapolis, and to JC Penney, and I had arranged for Walter Salmon, who was a senior Harvard professor in retailing, to be our lead. He traveled with us and interpreted what we heard.

We talked to the heads of each of those companies, had dialogues. I organized the trip so that each company would host us for a day, including meetings with the CEO and the management team. Over 45 people went to the seminar. We learned about the strategies of each of the companies and had the chance to ask questions about their direction and engage in discussion. Dayton Hudson was the dominant department store in Minneapolis, headed by Ken Dayton; one of their special features was their decision to give 5 percent of their profits each year to charity. Edison was a large shoe chain. They explained the concepts behind each of the chains they operated. Although they were a public company, they were managed by a member of the Edison family. JC Penney had a strong history from the time Mr. Penney started the company. They explained this to us and went on to discuss how they operate in malls and in smaller cities, and discussed their strong commitment to price and quality. In the evening, a few of us would exchange impressions of what we learned during the day before flying to our next stop. This was sort of an MBA program for those of us who never had an opportunity to have formal business education after we became CEOs and presidents.

That first seminar experience led to an extraordinary opportunity. The national YPO education chairman called from New York to talk to me. I was out of town, and I had a very creative secretary in those days. She took the call, and the chairman said that the Young Presidents were going to bring a seminar to the USSR. They wanted to talk to me about chairing that seminar; could I meet them in New York? My secretary, Candy, was very excited and said, "Oh, absolutely, I'll line it up and see that he's there." When she told me about it, I was a little appalled—how could I take that much time off?

But our business by that time was running smoothly. It was hard to imagine—just a few years before, Paul Harris had required my concentrated effort every day. I'd struggled to find staff who could take over any of my duties. But we had cleared that hurdle, at least for the time being, and come to the point where I could take on the exciting prospect of going to the USSR to chair a seminar.

I co-chaired the seminar the following year in June in the Soviet Union. The idea was to get 40 young capitalists to meet with Soviet officials and explore the ways we were running our businesses and, of course, how our countries were operating their economies. So I agreed to do this, and the first step was to take a preliminary trip. I went to Russia for a week in January after the Christmas season was over to make arrangements.

I flew into Moscow on a cold night. I was lucky—through some contacts, I arranged to have a professor involved with the Soviet Academy of Science who'd been to the United States several times meet me at the airport. He spoke perfect English. In Moscow a hotel room had been arranged for me. On the way into the heart of the city I noticed great big flags and banners with writing on them, and asked him what it all meant. "Oh," he said, "this means 'Things go better with Communism.' You know, in New York, you see 'Things go better with Coke'? This is our way of talking to our visitors."

I was taking some Russian lessons so that I could at least talk a little bit or know a few words, but that evening, at the restaurant, I had difficulty reading the menu. The waiter and I somehow figured out how to communicate, and he asked me where I was from. I said Indianapolis. Oh, he said, zzzzzzzzzz, and he made a gesture that meant he knew Indianapolis was known for car racing and the Indianapolis Motor Speedway. I thought that was really a start to learning about Russia.

I met with the various officials of interest who were going to be our hosts. After several days in Moscow, I traveled to Tbilisi, in the province of Georgia (one of our group stops). Air travel in the USSR was very different in the seventies. The seats were benches; no one fastened seat belts, and people walked around at all times during the flight. It was a unique experience.

Every night in the hotel in Tbilisi they had a band and dancing, and I noticed that mostly there were men dancing together and not with women. When I inquired about that, they said, "Oh, yes, would you like a woman to dance with you?" I said, "No, no." I never found out why there were so few women. But the men were all very friendly, and there were small tables of about seven or eight, and as I was their guest, they had a little Russian flag and a little American flag. They were really very welcoming in every way. I flew back to Moscow, then back to the United States, having arranged various meetings with various officials; I had even arranged for Khrushchev's son-in-law to be our opening speaker when the whole group got to Moscow.

In June, we set out with our wives—40 couples—on the trip. We made a number of interesting stops in Tashkent, Summerkand— where there were a lot of Muslims and Mosques—and Tbilisi and Kiev, and Leningrad. We had our own jet and a Russian crew. We had excellent food, and an excellent crew that spoke English, and we were really treated royally by Aeroflot, the Russian airline.

We were kept very busy. There was a banquet at noon and a banquet at night. We were given much too much food; I tried to explain that we really just wanted a small snack for lunch, and after several days I finally succeeded in doing that. We had been spending too much time in banquets and there were toasts and vodka. I couldn't really drink that much, but these people all drank a lot. We met with Communist Party officials, businesspeople, press people. One of those meetings back in Moscow was with the Novisty press agency, which had a reporter travel with us, who took lots of pictures and wrote a big article about us. In the United States there was also a picture in *Fortune* magazine.

The whole trip was most stimulating. Retailing in the Soviet Union then was very different from that in the United States. There was little merchandise and little choice. When there was merchandise, it was of low quality. In Tashkent, the temperature was ninety degrees. We looked at their key store, and they had fur hats and winter coats—no summer clothing whatsoever. I made inquiries, and they said that they didn't get any summer clothes this year, but maybe next year. Making a purchase in the Soviet Union required time and patience. Once you found something you wanted to buy, you had to find a person to hold it for you. Then you had to locate a special person who could look up the price and write it down for you. With this information, you went to a desk, paid for the purchase, took your receipt to another desk, and showed your receipt to get your merchandise. It was a very cumbersome process.

"Well," I thought, "How would it be if we had a Paul Harris store here to sell our off-price merchandise?" I told a couple of the kommissars, and they laughed, indicating how impossible this would be. Retailing in the Soviet Union was so far behind, so complicated, with such a limited amount of merchandise, that it really opened my eyes to how good we had it in the United States. We got each couple in the group to write about each day of our trip, and when we got home we had it published as a pamphlet with pictures, sketches, and observations.

A year later, Young Presidents asked me to head a seminar in Japan, and I gladly accepted. We started in Kyoto after the annual YPO University, which took place there, and traveled in the various cities around Japan—not Tokyo, just the smaller cities where Westerners were not yet common. We had interesting meetings with business and cultural people. That was a one-week trip, but there I learned a different phase of retailing. In Japan, they had small stores and very high per-square-foot productivity. Japan had a thriving economy. The selection and quality in Japan were high—just about the opposite of what I had seen the year before in the Soviet Union.

But unlike traveling in the USSR, changes on our itinerary were absolutely impossible. The Japanese had their agenda, and it had been agreed upon. Whereas in Russia I had been able to make a few changes, it was impossible in Japan. They didn't understand how to say no. It was always, "Oh yes, we can do that," and then they would give you fifteen reasons why you couldn't do that. But they would never give you no for an answer.

In Japan there were a few big department stores, and everyone bowed to you as you entered and again when you looked at products. I was particularly interested in their specialty store industry and had arranged some introductions. The discussions were one-sided. They had many questions and I was glad to answer. But while they asked me some questions about U.S. stores, every question I asked was deferred with, "Oh, yes, very interesting question, but information is not available now," and such. They were not open to sharing or exchanging information but obviously did a lot of business. The stores were usually narrow but three to five floors high.

Practically all the products were made in Japan, but nothing had content labels like we had in the United States, so I wasn't able to discern much information from that source, either.

These two trips convinced me of two things. Retailing is important anywhere in the world. But because of cultural differences, the experience of retailing in one country would probably make retailing very difficult to do in other countries. U.S. companies were leading the way into international commerce—particularly wholesale trade—but it seemed that retailing in other cultures might be impossible to arrange and manage.

The Young Presidents also took a family trip of 30 couples to Africa. I went with my wife and two daughters. We flew first to Dakar and down the western coast all the way to South Africa and came back through Ethiopia to Europe. This was a fascinating trip; we had interesting meetings with African government people and were hosted by our embassies.

As always in my travels, I kept my attention on retailing. In Dakar, on the first stop, we went to an open-air market and we saw many interesting things, but what caught my eye were some very colorful belts. I asked how much they cost, and the man said one dollar each. I thought, "What a great opportunity to import something unusual for our stores." So I said, "Okay, I would like to buy a hundred. How much can I save? What's your best price?" He looked at me and said, "Oh, a hundred. Big problem. I can make one, but a hundred, that's an awfully big problem. For a hundred, you would have to pay me a dollar fifty each." This was my first encounter where buying bulk cost me more, but it also gave me an insight into the economic situation that prevailed on the African continent. I did go ahead and buy a hundred of those belts and arranged to have them shipped. They were very unusual and I thought would make a great hit. When I put them in my stores, however, people looked at them, but didn't buy them. I ended up having to retail them for twenty-nine cents on a close-out. So that's another example of learning what's available overseas. We did buy some beautiful fabric, but more for personal consumption, not for business. This was another great opportunity to expand my horizons and include my family and learn about another part of the world.

Being president of a company has its advantages. Not everyone had the opportunity to take official trips to foreign lands. But I had built a good organization. They could function without me. A good leader does not make an organization dependent; that would ultimately be disastrous. A good leader develops people to do the job. I could leave for weeks and the organization would do well. In retrospect, it seems shocking that I was able to be away so much while Paul Harris grew—I was always so busy at home. But the business was getting along just fine without me.

YPO offered me another engaging opportunity back in the United States. As a result of contacts I made in the organization, I was invited to join the board of Upper Iowa College. I had never imagined I would have the chance to be a part of a university in this capacity. I had long pursued education any way I could, and had made a point of incorporating academic study into the business and our YPO seminars. Now I understood something about the way a college worked. I also made contacts there who would help Paul Harris later. And I continued, throughout my career, to incorporate both formal and experiential education into my life at the company.

All of these experiences were broadening, and as a result of the business and of being a member of the Young Presidents' Organization, I enlarged my horizons, had unique opportunities for learning, travel, meeting interesting people, and made great friends with stimulating people from all over the country. It was also a great way to learn and utilize my business to propel or enable me to make these contacts and to enrich my life with experiences I would never have imagined before.

CHAPTER SEVEN

Tornado: A Mixed Blessing

By THE LATE SEVENTIES, Paul Harris was established in the retail industry. We had come to be known to consumers and resources as a
solid organization. In 1976 we opened our one hundredth store, in
Columbia, Maryland. That completed 25 store openings for the year.
As American malls grew and prospered, so did Paul Harris. Columbia Mall was an unusual mall, which was developed as part of a
completely new suburb of Washington D.C. Our presence there was
an important milestone. We faced competition most directly from
The Limited and Casual Corner, both of which were larger than we
were. We had to work very hard to keep up with them; our growth
and success were fed by that competition in the malls.

I was traveling the world over with my buyers, envisioning and
ordering high-quality merchandise for our stores. We had built a
new headquarters office and distribution center in Indianapolis. In
1978, evolution, which I had so often sought out, was thrust upon
us.

We had moved into our new headquarters on Guion Road and
had broken ground for a large expansion because we were rapidly
running out of room for our growing operation. One Sunday in June,
I was visiting Washington, D.C., on a business trip. I had settled into
my hotel room to prepare for a long day of meetings.

The phone rang in the middle of the night. A voice on the other
end of the line told me that my entire company had been hit directly
by a tornado. I had a sinking feeling, like the beginning of the night-
mare when you feel you're falling, not knowing what will happen
when you hit the ground.

I thought, "Can this be real?"

It didn't seem possible.

A tornado had ripped through our headquarters. It was possible that everything was lost: buildings, offices, merchandise. No one would know the full extent of the damage for weeks. That phone call changed everything.

I spent the rest of the night on the phone, looking for flights and canceling the next day's business. The soonest I could get on a plane was morning. I'd have a whole night to lie awake imagining the disaster I'd find when I got home.

The tornado had destroyed homes and businesses through Indianapolis. Our new headquarters was decimated, and with it our entire season's merchandise. The storm tore right through one side of our existing distribution center and out the other and caved in the roof. It twisted the frame of our new construction beyond repair. It set off sprinklers throughout the facility, compounding structural damage with water damage. Luckily, since it was Sunday, nobody was in the building and no one was hurt.

So many things hung in tenuous balance. What do you do when the body of your work is destroyed? In spite of our hopes to the contrary, all of our merchandise was ruined. It was June, and we were staging new products for the fall. The flow of merchandise had begun to arrive in our warehouse; the upcoming sales season was nearly upon us. Teams outfitted in boots slogged through the water-soaked remnants and put merchandise into hampers. We thought maybe some could be dried and salvaged, but nothing could be saved.

After a couple of horrible days, we got the building cleared out. All of our computers were moved into trailers in the parking lot to be checked for water damage; we had to find out which of the disks were salvageable. After several days, we learned that some were damaged and some were not. We had another crew working in trailers in our parking lot, trying to determine the status of our merchandise. Merchandise stopped shipping to the stores: we had nothing to send. Everyone was nervous.

We began the process of dealing with our insurance company and turned our attention toward figuring out how to get back into business. We had a long rebuilding challenge ahead of us and would have to find a way to operate in the meantime. We had to figure out how to get new merchandise and ship it and process it to resume supplies to stores without a functional distribution facility. We found one vacant warehouse on the east side of Indianapolis that we could rent, provided we could get tables and equipment in. We benefited from the generosity that comes out in a crisis: some of our competitors helped us get right back on our feet, lending us supplies and equipment to build a makeshift operation. We set up a small facility across town from our Guion Road site, where we could begin to process merchandise until we determined the next steps.

We found a vacant distribution center more appropriate to our needs in New Jersey, and we leased it and made arrangements. Then, of course, we had to find and buy merchandise to ship and process. We were lucky. The incident was widely covered in the press, and most of our sources went out of their way to help us replenish or substitute merchandise. They also provided garment racks, boxes, and supplies to get us moving again. Within about ten days, we were able to get some flow back into our stores. This all took tremendous work. We had to process on our remaining computers what merchandise needed to be sent to what store. In 1978, we didn't have access to today's communication tools like email and the Internet; we had to put the information on planes and ship it to New Jersey. This was complicated and expensive. We had daily flights of information. We got a number of our people to volunteer to work there, supplemented their staff with local people, and after three or four weeks we had a semblance of an operation, though badly crippled, that would flow merchandise until we were able to rebuild.

Claiming insurance money to rebuild was complicated. We had a battle with our insurance company to determine fair replacement values for what was lost. They knew, of course, that it wasn't our fault, but it would be four to five months before we reached an agreeable settlement. Meanwhile, our banks helped us finance new inventory.

At the same time, we got busy figuring out how to reconstruct our building. Both our existing building and our new construction were destroyed. We had a steel frame for our expansion, but it didn't withstand the storm and would all have to be replaced. We had a hell of a mess for months.

Eventually, we got back on our feet. Our operations resumed, our stores were fully stocked, and tensions eased among our employees.

The damage the tornado had done to the property and the merchandise was obvious. But there was less tangible damage done, too. My partner, Earl Harris, decided that the retail business had gotten much more complicated and difficult than when we started out. His priorities had always been different from mine; the demands of growing the company had been wearing on him for years. The tremendous strain of recovery from the tornado had taken its toll: Earl was ready to retire.

He wanted to sell the company, but I couldn't imagine doing that. Paul Harris was my life. I had set out to build something, and I wasn't done. Though we were a public company, he and I were by far the major shareholders. We each held the same amount of stock. Even if I gathered every resource I had, I couldn't afford to buy him out.

We struggled to find a solution we could both live with. He could stay with the company, or I could decide to sell and stay with the new company. I worked around the different ideas and had lunch with the president of our local bank, which was our principal lender. He said, "If you're really determined, why don't you buy Earl out?" I told him I didn't have enough money, and he offered to lend it. I took every last dime my wife and I had, borrowed the rest from the bank, and made an offer to Earl. The bank must have had faith that I could be a viable customer again and was willing to back my buyout. Earl wanted mostly cash that he could use quickly, and he also wanted to remain on the board.

We reached an agreement, and in 1980, Earl left the company with money in his pocket and set up an office at Simon Property Group, owners and managers of the majority of shopping malls in North America. He and Mel Simon were good friends and had worked on a lot of real estate deals, setting our stores up in Simon malls. Simon was happy to have him join and made him a retail consultant. This turned out to be great for him, and he still has an office there. He was able to take some shares at Simon, all of which turned out positive for him. He invested the money I paid him, and our parting was amicable.

Earl's departure left me alone as the CEO of the company. I was very busy rebuilding and getting the company back on secure footing; the time I had available to oversee the development and purchase of our merchandise was shrinking. My most recent attempt to hire a merchandise manager, before the tornado, had again been unsuccessful. Finding talented people was and would always be the most pressing problem for Paul Harris, as it is for many businesses.

I had brought in a talented merchant from Marshall Field whose ideas were promising. But after a short time, employees began to come to my office with grievances. His management style was not what they were accustomed to; he yelled at them constantly.

When I brought it up to him, he said, "Why don't we build some padding around your office? That way you won't have to hear any of it."

I told him, "That's not a solution." From the start, I believed that employees should be treated humanely and fairly. It became obvious that he didn't feel the same. I had no choice but to let him go and decided to give the search a rest. Because of these personnel problems and not finding the right people, I was solely in charge of Paul Harris. My attention and time were splintered into all the facets of the company.

In 1980, I hired a talented manager named Rick Bomberger as director of stores. He came from the Gap, where he'd become a vice president at the age of twenty-nine. He did an exceptionally good job and pushed hard to expand the company more rapidly. I was most enthusiastic about the work he was doing, and three years later I made him president while I was chairman and CEO. I wanted to ensure that he would stay, so I arranged for him to purchase 23,000 shares of my stock at a private exchange rate much lower than market value. Our board of directors thought that was rather unusual and foolish—why should I offer mine instead of working something out through the company with more stock options? But I worried about competition raiding our staff and felt that this way he would really be tied in with me, and together we would do very well in the running of the company. We made that deal: over a three-year period he could exercise the option to purchase my stock at around three dollars a share, while our stock was selling at around sixteen dollars. So he was going to get a sweet deal and would be grateful and therefore more permanently tied to me and the company. This made me confident that he would stay with us. With his commitment, we would continue to grow and thrive, and I would have a talented, trustworthy key executive to run the operation of stores.

Once again the company had emerged from extremely difficult circumstances intact and improved. Challenge remained integral to our evolution. We began in the tornado's aftermath to push past the limitations of a recovering company into a new stage of growth. Our executive staff was now fully focused on this purpose, ready to move rapidly toward a new stage in the life of Paul Harris.

We came into the 1980s on strong, bullish footing. In January 1984, the *Indianapolis Business Journal* reported great news about the company in its 1983 Enterprise Awards. We had, despite "serious adversity" and reported losses in 1979 and 1981, come around to reporting consistent earnings. We hadn't seen a sales slump but had needed a reconfiguration of our administration and financial controls to offset the damage of the tornado and other factors. We had been criticized by stock analysts for our "spotty earnings pattern," a shortage of outstanding common stock, and the fact that we hadn't opened any new stores since 1979. The adversity we faced and the analytical practices we engaged made it possible to overcome, in time, each of the analysts' complaints. We were a new, streamlined, strong company on our way to what I was convinced was an amazing future.

CHAPTER EIGHT

A New Learning Curve: Self-Examination as a Way of Life and Leadership

EARL HARRIS'S DEPARTURE AND THE ESTABLISHMENT of his replacement were only a part of the sea change that was coming in Paul Harris's management.

Some of these changes were influenced by what I was learning outside of Paul Harris Stores. For some time, I had participated in a Harvard behavioral study led and reported by Professor Chris Argyris, who is now at MIT. The study was designed to examine the leadership tactics and styles of CEOs at a variety of U.S. companies and to encourage self-examination by its participants. The premise of the study was that there are two models for leadership behavior, which Argyris identified as "Model I" and "Model II." Both models were believed to produce fairly consistent results. The idea was that within the context of contemporary American business, it would benefit CEOs to examine their behavior and, for some participants, to initiate dramatic changes in style, attitudes, and practices.

Model I describes the traditional, authoritarian executive's behavior: he makes a decision and dictates what actions his employees will take. Employees expect to be given a set of orders to follow and are not in the habit of questioning their leader's decisions, contributing creatively to those decisions, or solving problems outside the parameters of the leader's established expectations.

Model II behavior is more complicated. Employees take ownership in decisions alongside their leaders; they are engaged in a more active and demanding role that requires them to be both creative and responsible, and to provide regular, sometimes confrontational feedback to their supervisors. Leaders have to encourage and engage this feedback, even when it feels threatening or ill-founded. They have to learn to trust their employees and to share their power. While Model I behavior was predicted to eventually lead to stagnation, Model II should produce fast-moving, visionary companies capable of sustained success.

I believed that changing Paul Harris's leadership behavior would benefit the company, and that implementing Model II behavior was suited to the kind of creative, exciting work I wanted to do. I felt that for Paul Harris to continue to grow and operate as a professional corporation, the work with Professor Argyris could help me be more competent and help the company. Further, if his predictions were correct, learning about Model II behavior should help me bring executives up in the company who could eventually take on increasingly responsible roles.

Earl Harris, who was still with the company when the study began, declined to take part. His reaction was, "I'll be damned if I'm going to have a subordinate tell me what to do or how to behave," a good example of Model I behavior. So I embarked on this adventure on my own.

Seven men, each the head of his company, joined in the study. We met for three or four days per session four times a year with two professors to evaluate our behavior in our organizations and to discuss it in an attempt to learn to improve. At our first meeting with Professor Argyris in Acapulco we decided to invite our wives to one of our sessions during the week. We were there for six days and had signed up to meet six mornings that week. On the fifth morning, our wives attended. Professor Argyris went around the room and asked each wife how she had been invited by her husband. Practically every wife simply stated that her husband had told her to come to the meeting. The professor explained that this was Model I, authoritarian behavior. In short, the wives had been coerced to attend, whereas in Model II, discussion would have taken place examining why it would be useful to attend and creating a consensus.

In theory, Model II leadership behavior suited my entrepreneurial spirit and openness to change. Our executives participated in a component of the study designed to learn about enacting behavioral changes organization-wide. These changes weren't easy. What was easy was dishing out directions and never being challenged. But Professor Argyris advocated Model II leadership practices, and I believed his claim that it would work best in an entrepreneurial, fast-moving, innovative company.

Internal changes could sometimes cause conflict; even with good intentions it was easy to revert to old ways. Subordinates had been used to following orders. When they were invited to participate, sometimes they had trouble trusting the invitation. It was harder for them, too, so it became a total cultural change.

I was excited about participating in the project in part because I understood that in order for the company to grow, I needed key employees who could question and confront me. I hoped to cultivate people who could, over time, take on more and more responsibility. I saw the study as a way to help me make that happen.

Changing one's behavior is much easier said than done. I was surprised at how hard it was. The seven CEOs had a method for implementation: each participant would tape meetings with executives. During our get-togethers, we would play the tapes and discuss with our consultant what went wrong. Usually something went wrong. The group worked for over four years. Most of us thought, in all that time, that we were only marginally successful. Different CEOs would come to the meetings with different problems. We would bring our tapes, confident that when we reviewed them, we had done well, and the rest of the group would point out all the Model I behavior evident in each encounter. This was frustrating to us all.

Argyris's book *Increasing Leadership Effectiveness* reports details about our participation, with our names changed for anonymity. But for me, the study was about more than academic findings. I was learning about *myself* from unexpected sources. Paul Harris executives were encouraged to confront me with their observations about my decisions and about my leadership; we were to establish a less hierarchical dialogue than we'd been engaged in for years.

I learned just how far from the second model of behavior I'd been, even when I thought I was performing well. Employees sometimes found themselves confused by the different approaches and philosophies Earl and I presented as I attempted to change. They felt they were sometimes caught up in our conflicts. Though I thought I'd made myself available, asking to hear all kinds of good and bad news, they wished I had been more open. This is a very hard lesson. We all have a view of ourselves, and denial and self-deception prevent us from seeing the truth of our vision. It is crucial for a CEO to have a trusted person who they know can and will speak the truth.

As predicted, management behavioral change was tricky to implement. If those who reported to me looked to me for initiative, and I was reluctant to stand on firm ground and provide traditional, decisive leadership, many wouldn't know where to turn. On the other hand, if I continued to lead in a Model I mode, employees would be hesitant to change their own behavior. But the study itself, and my coming to understand that different approaches can work, taught me a number of things about my own leadership style, and it reminded my employees that I was committed to making Paul Harris the best company it could be and to being the best boss possible.

Since that time, I have asked myself, "Did this really help or hurt me in running the company?" I'm glad I did it, but to this day, I'm not sure it was the best choice. Sometimes people who tended to Model I behavior had simple lives. Model II behavior made life complicated. And it wasn't useful for everyone.

Jan Woodruff, a VP who dealt regularly with vendors and whom I most often turned to for honest feedback, was one example. If a shipment of dresses did not fit properly, she would need to find a way to return them for credit and not put them into our stores. But the dress vendors were a tough group and did not want to face up to the fact that their companies had made mistakes. They would carry on and yell that she was trying to take advantage of them. Model II required an honest discussion of the facts in order to find a solution, but the dress people wanted no part of a discussion of the facts and believed that by being loud and yelling they could avoid the problem. Jan felt that she needed to act in an unreasonable manner as well, à la Model I, to resolve the issue. This required a behavior inconsistent with a fair and honest examination of the situation, and she had to work that way to do her job well. She could not shift to a different behavior in her internal dealings in our organization. She felt that this was the world that existed in the industry, and she had to live with it and operate within it.

All of Paul Harris's executives had the option to participate or not. Most did; I expect that some wished to abstain but felt pressured by my own commitment to the project. I admired Jan for having the guts to say she wouldn't participate. But I think it's fair to say that everyone at the company struggled as much as I did. On the one hand, I had to be a leader and take responsibility for the company's direction; on the other, it was important to avoid being so authoritarian. I worried that people would wonder, "What's he up to?" Sometimes I felt I was damned if I did, damned if I didn't.

But there were situations where applying Model II principles made a clearly positive difference in our company. In one example, a conflict came up with a promising merchandise manager I had hired from Nieman Marcus. He was a very personable guy. But after a buying trip he'd taken to Europe with some staff members, several of the buyers, all women, came to tell me that he had made passes at them, trying to enter their hotel rooms in the middle of the night and initiating totally inappropriate contact. They told me they'd never go on a trip with him again. They ended the discussion by asking what I planned to do about it.

They were right: I had to make a choice about how to handle the situation. I talked to the manager. He pooh-poohed the complaints. I clearly couldn't come to an easy resolution this way.

Model II required that I get everyone together to get all the perspectives on the table, lay them out in front of everybody, and come to a resolution. At the meeting, the manager maintained his dismissive attitude, but the women were adamant: his behavior hadn't seemed meaningless to them. He made a series of lame excuses, but it became more and more apparent during the meeting that the buyers had legitimate complaints and shouldn't have to travel with him again. I had to ask for his resignation. Though this presented a real dilemma, it resolved the situation far more efficiently and honestly than any effort to make an authoritarian decision based on a he-said-she-said discussion could have.

All these years later, I'm still glad I pursued the study and worked to change my behavior. It was incredibly hard work, and it often made me less self-assured within my company. But it made me more open-minded, too; it was an arduous, important part of the personal growth I pursued all through my career.

Model II behavior came to represent an ideal, a goal for many situations. Of course I had already known that innovation required employees who felt welcome to be creative and even confrontational. I had been a part of this kind of collaboration time and again on our many merchandise development trips, as I developed seasoned buyers and came to rely on their insights for each new line. But Professor Argyris's study challenged me to take that same attitude into the company's larger culture, to learn its advantages and difficulties, and to be articulate and thoughtful in its application in everyday situations.

Chapter Nine

Introducing Pasta: Italian Street Clothing

THE 1980s SAW TREMENDOUS ENERGY at Paul Harris. We had left the seventies with a redesigned operation and consistently positive annual sales and profits. Our entrepreneurial culture had brought us success, and that success, in turn, enabled us to continue innovating.

The growth of Paul Harris reflected and was partially fueled by dramatic shifts in American culture and society, particularly in the roles women occupied in professional and social spheres. The push for women's rights in the seventies had produced real, culture-changing results by this time. Women were no longer struggling to get into the workplace. They were now pushing for equality *within* the workplace, discovering the glass ceiling, and devising ways to push against it.

All this change manifested itself dramatically in the fashion and apparel world. Women's lives required two wardrobes: one for days and another for evenings and weekends. Further, working women's struggle for equal position and pay as men had unofficially established a tailored, coordinated dress code. Paul Harris's Haberdasher line—the predominant component of our offering—suited the working woman well. But it failed to draw the mall shopper searching for casual wear into our stores.

We had a casual line featuring jeans and shirts called Red Mountain Clothing Company, but it was limited in its scope. The same changes in the culture that brought women into the workforce had energized their social lives as well and given them more options. Our customers in their twenties and thirties weren't necessarily shopping for a married lifestyle. Women were active in a broader range of social activities than they'd ever been; this demanded a more vibrant, fun clothing choice than we offered. Fashion magazines, television, and the media in general emphasized the distinction, presenting stark differences between workplace and casual selections.

We recognized this need as an opportunity and hired a creative consultant named Mike Shaw to develop a concept to give our customers—our bosses—the casual options they needed. We wanted to develop an entirely different concept from the one Paul Harris stood for and felt a fun, colorful, casual product line would be perfect. We devoted tremendous energy to the development of that line, playing with many ideas. One such proposal, Guerilla, focused on street wear. The idea was edgy and new, but not right for us. We felt that Italian street clothing—loose, colorful, and easy-care—was the way to go. We finally agreed upon a concept we called Pasta; it was one of the most exciting innovations of my career.

There are three ways to grow a business. One is to increase the amount of money being spent in the type of stores you already have. This could involve convincing new customers to buy from existing stores or expanding the number of stores to gain access to new customers. A second way is to sell more of what you have or invent new products to sell to your current customers. For example, if you sell women's clothing, you could add accessories. A third option is to buy or create a totally new chain or product line independent of your established offering. A contemporary example would be The Limited, which at one time had The Limited targeted for the 25–35-year-old woman, Lane Bryant geared toward women 35 and over, Limited Too for 5- to 15-year-olds, and Limited Express aimed at the 15–25 set.

The focus of Pasta was fun, attention-getting, comfortable clothes. It was made to appeal to our core customer but was not serious clothing. Pasta had more detail, and may even have been a little gimmicky. It was a way for a woman to express her individuality and was geared to please her and maybe her husband or boyfriend, but not her boss. It was designed to appeal to emotion, not to be understated or classic like Paul Harris's Haberdasher. The priority was look, then price, then quality. It had to have a high degree of easy care, functionality, and emotionality because it was to be worn frequently. It had to be washable and stand up; our customers didn't want to spend money on dry cleaning for leisure clothes. We established an order of importance for the line: knit tops, then pants, sharp accessories, jackets, shirts, and shorts.

We liked the name Pasta because it expressed freedom and it had an Italian slang to it. We said that Pasta must be run like a newspaper, with a constant flow of newness, and be distinct from the fashion orientation of Paul Harris. Because it was colorful it would enliven our stores. We wanted novelty and a keen sensitivity to change in Pasta products. The Pasta customer's chronological age was not important, though the Paul Harris core customer age range was 18–35. Like other Paul Harris lines, Pasta had a color palate for each season, but because color was a key ingredient, the Pasta color palette was always very different from the Paul Harris lines.

We had the experience of successfully developing brand identity with our logo in the 70s. Retail expert and former board member Liz Kraft-Meek would later say that with that logo and the accompanying concepts, we were doing better than anybody in specialty retail. Our rainbow logo had become recognizable everywhere we had a presence, so we knew how to invent a new brand with similar results. We had even revised that logo, changing its colors to reflect a less cutting-edge style without threatening its recognizability or brand integrity. So we felt we had a good idea of how to establish a brand.

Pasta's launch attracted fabulous newspaper publicity. We launched in Indianapolis and had a full-color page in the *Indianapolis Star.* The *Detroit News* had a color picture and said "Pasta going noodles over tasty clothes." Another paper headlined it, "Paul Harris line adds a dash of Italiano and tasty new clothes called Pasta."

The publicity fed the food metaphor, and we had some ideas the creative consulting agency developed as well, centered around the slogan "Very tasty clothes." We had linguini corduroy pants, ziti jeans, tortellini tops, and so on. "Going noodles for tasty clothes" was a key feature. Other slogans included: Pasta has color, not calories. Satisfy a craving: Have Pasta. Give in to an urge: Have Pasta.

Instead of kisses, have Pasta. Famished? Have Pasta. Don't Starve. Have Pasta. Don't deny yourself. Have Pasta. We had promotional ideas, too. We developed a Pasta T-shirt: One for you, Pastabella, the second for your Pasta Fella. A very tasty T is free with any purchase over $33. We had the Pasta Look-book Cookbook. Because we tied it into food as well as fun, Pasta really turned me on. The work satisfied my creativity, and we did a lot of unusual things. We had unique fixtures and signage for the stores. Our offering of patterned sweaters, graphic T-shirts, and other casual wear really appealed to a creative customer, and we found that we didn't have to mark Pasta items down as frequently as other Paul Harris lines. We did a lot of posters. Pasta quickly became my favorite; it was our most creative endeavor yet.

We opened a Pasta section in one corner of every Paul Harris store. In only a few weeks, it became apparent that we had something cooking here. We decided we had to do more. We told our real estate specialist to look for smaller spaces in malls and opened Pasta stores, if possible next door to Paul Harris, but where that wasn't possible, freestanding. Some of the Pasta stores were much smaller than Paul Harris, approximately, 1200 to 1800 square feet, and the rent was higher per square foot, but Pasta was producing more dollars per square foot than Paul Harris. By late 1980 we had 86 separate Pasta stores.

In a short period of time, it became clear that we needed separate buyers for Pasta. We established a group of creative young women to develop the Pasta line. The new group included my oldest daughter, Eloise. Eloise had joined our company reluctantly a year before; she had wanted to maintain a professional identity separate from the company, confident that all her successes were a result of her work, not her name. We took precautions: she didn't report to me, and wasn't promoted by me. If anything, I was less indulgent of Eloise than of other employees. I was harsh about her work—no doubt overly so. I'm sure this made her job difficult, but I wanted to be certain that no one could say I favored my daughter in the company. Some tension existed between us, and in later years when she was promoted by another executive, she found herself reporting to me. We often disagreed. But the conflict trained her as a focused, sharp merchant.

She came to Paul Harris from a shoe company in California, where her work was rigidly structured. Our company's environment was a bit of a culture shock. She'd come from a place where a buyer had a specific goal to meet, and any major alterations in strategy or procedure were a result of missing that goal. The forward-thinking, fast-paced Paul Harris workplace was both startling and exciting. She developed and bought knits for Paul Harris successfully but found the company to be less friendly than the one she'd left. At the shoe company, most of her social contacts had been co-workers. At Paul Harris, she would have only one close friend.

Although Paul Harris was not a family business—it was a public company—we had a majority stock ownership, and I was the board chair and CEO. I had seen too many family-run businesses that ran into trouble when their children came on board, so I had been somewhat hesitant to hire my daughter. She had done well at the shoe chain, where she had been promoted from store manager to buyer. One of our board members had heard about her success and suggested that we bring her in. My first reaction had been mixed at best. I didn't want "family" as part of our company and was afraid it would inhibit our younger people. On the other hand, she had demonstrated real aptitude, and the idea had appeal.

Eloise, too, was afraid people would think she was a spy. After months of dialogue, the board made her an offer; with the help of her mother, whose enthusiasm about having her back in the city was persuasive, we convinced her to join Paul Harris.

Eloise established her place at Paul Harris with the development of Pasta. She and her close friend in the company bought exclusively for Pasta. With the division of duties came a split in culture that mirrored the distinctions between the clothing lines: the Pasta buyers thought the Haberdasher lines were stuffy and boring; Haberdasher buyers thought Pasta was a bit too wild. The Pasta buyers developed their own color range, traveled separately, and went to the Orient separately; in a way, we began to have an internal competition between Paul Harris and Pasta. Of course, Haberdasher was still our mainstay, but Pasta was growing rapidly and making money. The Pasta buyers entertained risky novelty items, many of which never made it to the sales floor. For example, they were thinking of underpants printed with a pasta sauce spill; Eloise, who bought knits, disliked the idea but was encouraged to check it out. Along with some of the other edgy novelties, it was eventually rejected. They bought other novelty and graphic items that were highly successful.

Pasta's dramatic achievements fueled growth throughout the company. In 1985 we reported an increase in earnings of 18 percent, and in 1986, 20 percent. We had a more geographically diverse presence and had built an organization made up of experienced, accomplished people. We were bullish and aggressive and began to feel that we could do no wrong.

Meanwhile, we were facing a specific set of challenges brought on by the explosion of Pasta. In effect, we had two creative companies with very different ideas functioning under one umbrella. We were still lacking a key head merchant to coordinate, oversee, and direct both of these companies. My overall leadership allowed even less time for direct merchandising since Earl Harris's departure. We also had to find a way to promote both lines simultaneously. We developed material to pass out: one side said, "Trust yourself, try new things, wear Pasta," and on the other side, we would say "Dress with style," "Wear our clothes with confidence," or "How do you shop with style? You'll see at Paul Harris."

The separate creative staffs had particular struggles, too. The lines had distinct target customers: Paul Harris's target was the working woman who dressed practically and conservatively and was price-conscious. We excelled in quality for the money and had a good following. Pasta, on the other hand, was geared to the adventurous young woman who wanted to dress colorfully and have fun. The lines each had a very different approach, and often, although they were sold either by the same salespeople or in neighboring stores, customers looking for a specific item weren't likely to buy from both lines. So, for example, only one line could carry a particular item. If Eloise, as a knits buyer for Pasta, wanted turtlenecks to accentuate her sweater lines, she had to make them dramatically different from Paul Harris's turtlenecks. While these kinds of conflict were relatively minor and usually solved through creativity, they were systematic. We needed greater control.

Although we were the company I'd always wanted Paul Harris to be—growing, creative, exciting—I decided it was time to institute some procedures to make certain our momentum wasn't taking us away from our customer-based focus. I was committed to constant re-examination, and wanted to be sure our next steps were based on knowledge, not just inertia. I hired a retail consulting firm, Cheskin + Masten, to conduct an evaluation and study of our company. They'd just done an impressive study for Pepsi Cola, and proposed several options to learn more about our business. They conducted a series of focus group studies that were well ahead of their time for specialty retailers—the kind of studies that retailers began conducting in the late 1990s and continue to take on now. Focus groups are the dominant research technique in product marketing. In a focus group small groups of consumers are guided by a professional moderator in a discussion about a product or service.

Focus groups are used to see what consumers think, how they feel. The name of the retail game is understanding the customer better than the competition. If you understand the consumer, you can give them what they want, when they want it, and in the way they want it better than the competition.

Cheskin + Masten recruited Paul Harris customers representative of each of our regions, various age groups, and divergent lifestyles. We sat behind two-way mirrors while they showed customers our best-selling items, worst-selling items, and items we were considering for upcoming seasons. We watched while our core customers taught us how to merchandise our stores.

One of the great mistakes that business executives make is talking only to one another. Executives live the business, and their view of what is important may sometimes be very different from what their customers think. Our focus groups led to many confirmations of our expectations and some surprises. We found that, for example, a top-selling pair of Pasta orange shorts was of little interest to the typical Paul Harris customer. We knew that someone was buying them, but to our chagrin, we didn't know who. It appeared that we had developed an entirely different constituency who bought Pasta apparel. As a result, we worked to move the Pasta line closer to the range of appeal of the customers we studied. In addition to focus groups, the consultants had a new and interesting technique. They asked participants to take photos of their homes—their families, their closets. The reasoning was that this would lead to a view of how our customer lived that could not be learned from surveys and focus groups. This was a modern-day anthropological investigation. We couldn't live with the customers we were studying, but we could see their things. We got to look into the closets and homes of the women who shopped at our stores. Paul Harris was never a company that purported to dictate fashion to its customers, but rather wished to anticipate their needs and provide apparel that fit their lives. To do that, we needed to know much more than what they liked to wear. We learned where they worked, what kind of leisure activities they loved, who they really were.

The study had two important results. First, the researchers used the information to develop profiles of two hypothetical women who were likely to purchase our merchandise. They called these woman Susan and Lynn; they were fictionalized composites of many of the study participants. Susan represented a young-in-spirit single woman with an active lifestyle. She was divorced, in her late twenties to early thirties, worked full-time, and spent time dating and with friends. Lynn was a thirty-something married mother of two whose lifestyle centered around her family and her home. She was a busy full-time mother who had left a teaching career to be with her children. While these two prototypes obviously could not represent every woman who shopped at Paul Harris and Pasta, they were compiled to embody the range of tastes and lifestyles we thought our customers had. We developed merchandise, store design principles, and sales staff training based both on their divergent styles and on the many shopping preferences they shared, such as well-lighted, easy-to-shop stores and well-matched clothing options.

I was impressed by what this research could do to help our business. It reinforced my belief that self-examination is critical for business. This regular self-examination continued to be a normal part of what we did.

There were still challenges and opportunities to do better, as always, and there were tremendous storms on the horizon. But the company we built had evolved into something enormously powerful, with a life and momentum of its own, and we had taken steps to understand that momentum and to take on our growth and development with a greater insight than ever before.

We had learned more about our customers than we had ever imagined, but we had also learned, as Pasta continued to grow, about the excitement and danger of pursuing great ideas to their fullest height. Pasta was one of the brightest stars of Paul Harris's life span, but it stretched the limits of our merchandising oversight impossibly thin and threatened the company's unity as it ascended. Once again, I risked getting too caught up in the creative elements of the company. And while it appeared to be serving us well at the time, the focus groups illustrated the extent to which we had drifted away from our goals. We weren't even sure who our Pasta customer was; how could we continue to effectively anticipate her needs? We had to understand our customer to be able to repeat and prolong our success. After the study, we began to reel the Pasta line in so that we could establish its appeal to the Paul Harris customer we knew we could count on.

CHAPTER TEN

Heading Off the Rails

As Pasta became a phenomenon, other forces also spurred our growth onward. During the mid- to late eighties, what we now call consumer confidence was high. Our target customer was a woman between the ages of 18 and 35. These women were experiencing an economic boom. Many were from dual-income families. They needed a wardrobe to work and a wardrobe to play and had disposable income from which to build that wardrobe.

Meanwhile, shopping had become something of a national pastime; while husbands watched football and baseball, women were shopping in the malls. Most importantly, there were few other retailers specializing in developing merchandise to serve our core customer.

The 1980s were an incredibly optimistic time for the company. In June 1987, the company was doing so well that the board declared a 3-for-2 stock split for shareholders. We told people that it reflected the growth of the business as well as our confidence in the future. We also added three new directors to our board. One was Liz Kraft, a retail expert at Simon Properties. Another was Jim Gordon, who was on the board of Liz Claiborne. He was in the piece goods business, and helped us better understand fabric quality, pricing, and negotiation. Scott Hodes, an attorney in Chicago, had taken an interest in the company for some time and joined us as well. Building our board of directors was an ongoing effort; I worked continuously to make sure it was populated by people who could help us with their expertise and connections in the retail industry. Each new addition made us smarter and more capable.

We took on several projects to support the staff and organization as a whole, including the production of recruiting and internal documents that helped keep everyone involved in our culture of change and energy. One such document, a brochure called "Paul Harris Stores, Inc. CULTURE," laid out explicitly our philosophy for internal communication for our associates. We wanted to establish a closer rapport with those associates and to communicate our commitment to eleven specific values. We also developed "Do you really know Paul Harris?" which was designed to demonstrate visually and verbally to our associates who we were, what we stood for, and especially the difference between our Pasta and Paul Harris strategies in the stores. As the retail industry in the 1980s became ever more competitive, we wanted to create and ensure a solid understanding of our company with our associates. Poaching of sales associates from one chain to another was becoming commonplace. Pat Nolan, who came up in the company first as a store manager, then as a regional manager, reported far less turnover than industry averages throughout the eighties. These brochures were part of a program to make our associates feel a deeper connection to the company.

Among the many forces at Paul Harris during that decade were significant influxes of cash and the establishment of a nearly complete staff of talented, experienced people. All of these forces converged along with the immediate success of Pasta to encourage us forward in a dizzying, electrifying expansion.

One of the interesting things that happens when you are successful is that you begin to attract attention. The first time this happens, you don't think of it as a potential vulnerability. A curious situation turned into our first big boon. A chain of department stores in Iowa called Younker Brothers started buying some of our public stock. I called the principal. He explained that since the department store business is very static, they had decided to research some specialty stores and invest some money in one of them to offset the department store business. After looking at several companies, they liked Paul Harris. He said, "We like what you're doing and how you're doing it, so we allocated several million dollars to invest in your stock. We have no interest in running it, we only hope that with time our stock will continue to do well and be profitable, and give us a good handle on being a part of the specialty business."

I was a little suspicious, but they seemed to be decent people. They didn't give us any problems, they didn't ask to be on our board, and there was nothing I could do about it anyway. It didn't appear to be headed toward any kind of buyout or takeover; we were simply in the odd situation of having a department store own a chunk of our stock.

After a year or two, Younkers was bought by a very large insurance company named Equitable of Iowa that was headquartered in Des Moines. Equitable of Iowa bought Younker Brothers as an investment in their portfolio. With that purchase, they inherited Paul Harris stock and didn't quite know what to do with it. They had been interested in the stable Iowa department store chain and weren't interested in the more dynamic specialty retail business.

Equitable didn't want our stock, and their treasurer proposed selling it. I wasn't very keen on having our stock dumped on the market; they owned enough to drop our value. At the same time, we were continuing to expand and it became clear that we really needed more money to continue. The treasurer of Equitable and I had served together on the board of directors of Upper Iowa University; this familiarity helped us to make agreeable arrangements. I asked if Equitable would be a part of a public offering, which would allow them to sell the stock on the market without producing a subsequent drop in its value. That appealed to them, and because they were a well-respected insurance company, they had good contacts on Wall Street. This connection put Paul Harris in a good position to find a company to present our public offering.

In the summer of 1983, we made an arrangement to bring 880,000 shares into the market. Equitable sold 489,000 shares, which was their part, and I sold 69,000 shares. The sale, almost 30 years after I started the company, was my first profit draw—it gave me my first financial independence from the company. The rest of the offering was sold by the company. It left me with 672,000 shares, or 28 percent of the ownership of the company, which of course was not the majority, but my attorneys felt would ensure my having control. More importantly, the offering brought enough cash into Paul Harris to sustain our continued growth.

We were very bullish and aggressive and began to feel that we could do no wrong. At the time of the offering, we operated 172 stores, of which the majority were Paul Harris stores, but forty-one stores were budget stores in strip centers. They were mostly in Indiana, with twelve in Ohio and one in Illinois. The offering price of shares was twelve dollars per share. For years, from the day we started, we had used a local accounting firm, Katz Sapper. Irwin Katz was on our board and was a very close advisor and a friend. However, when we proceeded toward the offering with the underwriter, Paine Webber, they insisted that our books be audited by a national accounting firm, and much to my regret, we could only use Katz for our tax filings. We hired Price Waterhouse to be the national firm. That really wasn't my desire, but I had no choice—it was a side effect of our expanded operation. The offering required tremendous amounts of meetings and paperwork. It monopolized our time, but when we finally concluded, we all felt very good about accomplishing another milestone in the development and growth of Paul Harris.

By this point, we were showing up on a number of radar screens. One of these screens belonged to Milton Petrie of Petrie Stores. Petrie was a large, successful chain operation. Mr. Petrie began to pursue us in 1985 and wanted me to sell him the company. Mr. Petrie and his company were very influential in the industry. I had no interest in selling and told him so, but he was not going to be denied and pursued me relentlessly. We had lunch whenever I was in New York. A few years before, he had pursued and bought Toys"R"Us, which turned out to be a wonderful investment for him. He liked what he had heard about our company, and thought he could make a killing with us, as he had with Toys"R"Us.

Over our meetings, he showed himself to be an unusual man with an interesting sense of humor. On one visit, he said to me, "I want you to meet some of my girls." He meant his key executives. They were vice presidents, ages 72 and 74.

Our luncheons were very pleasant, but I told him I did not wish to sell. He thought I was bargaining for a better price, and after about nine months of pursuing me, he finally looked at me and said, "I guess you really don't want to sell. You're an entrepreneur, just like me."

I said, "Milton, you got it."

He still wanted to own a piece of the company. He proposed to invest ten million dollars in stock.

Ten million dollars in new capital was enticing. I hired a top-notch lawyer, Klaus Eppler of Proskauer & Rose, to draw up a demanding contract: Milton would not be on our board, he could not tell me what to do, he had to vote with me on all issues, and he could not interfere in any way or talk to any of our executives. I didn't expect him to agree. But he had made up his mind that he wanted a piece of Paul Harris, and after a few negotiations, he agreed and signed the contract. We had ten million dollars in new capital in 1986.

After Milton bought the stock, he stuck to the agreement, but he would call me every few weeks, checking in. He'd mention a center where we both had stores, wanting to compare results. If the center's Paul Harris store wasn't doing as much business as he was, he'd say, of our manager, "Fire the bitch."

Another windfall in the eighties resulted from a merchandising relationship. We made most of our products ourselves overseas, but we also kept looking for unusual vendors in the United States. My daughter, Eloise, who was in charge of the Pasta line, found a vendor in California named Marci & Me and started doing a lot of business with them. They had a unique, colorful, fresh approach, and she bought some of their products and got them to make special products just for us.

Eloise was very enthusiastic about Marci & Me. She worked successfully with them for quite some time and wanted me to meet the principal to see if we could develop a closer relationship. Alan and Marci Polanski owned the company. We had a series of very good meetings, and they said they would enjoy making special items for us. They were manufacturing mostly overseas, but in order for them to expand, they asked us to consider investing some money to guarantee their line of credit. So we proceeded and worked up a detailed arrangement for compensation.

Their designer, Patrick, came to Indianapolis several times. For a year or two, this was a great combination, and we were very happy with the collaboration. They supplemented our ability to develop Pasta products, and we utilized their design expertise and production know-how in the Orient to supplement ours. After a couple of years, though, they decided they would move in a different direction, to be less colorful and vibrant, to go after what is known as the missy market. That wasn't at all what Pasta was about. We tried for a few months to find a way to make the relationship work but found they no longer made the kind of products that belonged in our Pasta line.

I proposed to the principals that we part company in a friendly manner. With some negotiations, they bought our interest out. Paul Harris made a fair amount of money in that investment and we separated ways.

In the meantime, we had been negotiating with Prudential for a ten-year, twenty-million-dollar loan. Our board felt that the time to secure money was when you don't need it. We weren't hungry for money but knew we wanted to keep on growing. Our board felt we should pursue the financing because when you really need money it tends to be difficult to get.

Bill Haberle, a professor emeritus at Indiana University's Kelley School of Business, has a theory about this kind of situation: it's possible that the leaders who excel at running a tight, frugal ship are not equipped to lead a company with cash into its future. He guesses correctly that the money was burning holes in our pockets. We couldn't wait to apply it to our already steady upward momentum.

While our real estate team established locations for our new Pasta stores, they were also growing the roster of Paul Harris stores. Our geographic reach and sales figures were bigger than ever. Every day we were doing more, and doing it better. On our quarterly report in 1986, we reported an increase of 20 percent, and in 1985 an 18 percent increase in earnings; we had more geography and had successfully brought experienced people into the company. We had two creative companies with very different ideas, but it gave us an opportunity to expand more rapidly, which we did—which in turn started to create a lot of new problems for us that had to be managed and dealt with.

Our buyers were still traveling the world to develop ideas, and I was traveling all over the country to visit our new stores as well as continuing overseas buying trips. We added locations in the southeast and southwest and developed a greater presence in regions where Paul Harris stores already existed. The broadened area where we operated went as far as Denver, into Michigan, Florida, and Boston. We were now covering a very large area. While we were successful and riding high, it did occur to me that we needed to take some safeguards and check whether we were on target, and if we weren't, figure out how to adjust or improve. This was when we hired Cheskin + Masten to study our customers.

We were operating three different divisions, Paul Harris, Pasta, and 5 to 20, a reincarnation of our budget store, for a total of 273 stores by 1986. We were growing too rapidly. We had added nineteen stores in 1984, thirty-five in 1985; fifty in 1986, and sixty-five stores during 1987. As I look back upon it, that was no doubt too rapid, but we felt we were doing most things right. We still needed merchandise talent and kept looking for it, but we were profitable and growing. We were gung-ho to continue expanding and could see no clouds in the sky.

As we added stores we kept an eye toward making sure our stores had a unique and interesting look. As well as we were doing, it was important that we continue to attract new shoppers from the malls into our stores. I was particularly taken by the look of a chain of stores in London. I inquired who had designed these stores and found out a firm named David Davis was doing it. I contacted them and invited them to Indianapolis to spend a few days looking at our stores. Could they do something to make us stand out in the mall? They said absolutely, and we hired them. This was quite an undertaking to bring in a group of English design people. They were young and creative. They made many trips. It took our construction people a lot of coordination, but they did design a very unique-looking store. Of course, I loved it because it was new, different, and challenging and would help move us forward into a new era of retailing, which is exactly what I was constantly striving for. I made many trips to London, became friendly with the designers, and found the process very exciting. Many specialty stores look to Europe for merchandise ideas, and we'd been doing so for years, so it was not a unique thing for us to look there for architects. We launched our redesign effort in 1986. It was an exciting endeavor, but also a taxing and expensive undertaking.

Rick Bomberger was doing a great job and pushing to continue expansion. I was still serving as both CEO and chief merchandising manager; I worried about being able to manage continued expansion effectively, as that expansion made buying our merchandise increasingly complicated. But I went along with our plans, and we expanded rapidly through the eighties to 1991. We were opening stores at too brisk of a rate. I remember one meeting on a Saturday morning where eighty-six potential new locations were proposed by our real estate department, and I really felt uncomfortable. How could we deal with that many different situations? My head was beginning to spin. But some of our younger people were really enthusiastic. Our VP of real estate said they were great locations, great deals. It turned out that was an overstatement. We laid the foundation of overexpansion. We were too ambitious, and trying to do it all too fast.

Bill Haberle has also said that the management team that successfully runs a small-to-midsized organization isn't necessarily cut out to take on a larger operation. During our supercharged expansion, we had doubled the number of stores under the Paul Harris umbrella. Our team, so recently certain we could do no wrong, was badly overextended. Many of our real estate choices began to look like mistakes; appealing locations had been contractually tied to poor ones in several deals. We had signed leases we should have considered more critically. We didn't have the infrastructure to handle that many new stores, that many locations. I felt uncomfortable, but I did go along with our ambitious staff to approve it. I know now that I should have spoken up and said, "Let's slow down." But the fact is, I didn't want to stand in the way. I too was excited. We began to run into a period where business was generally off.

We still had problems with creative oversight, as well. As CEO, I was heavily focused on the expansion efforts. Our years-long struggle to find the right person to oversee our merchandising decisions was coming to a point of crisis. We had studied our customers so that our people could have a definite consumer in mind when they were looking to develop products. We also used that knowledge to help store managers identify who customers might be and what to expose them to. But with the overexpansion, our geographic reach was problematic. Some of the markets had different shopping habits. The one that caused the most trouble was the south. Southern shoppers had a different lifestyle and different needs. What stands out, of course, is that Paul Harris had become known for unique novelty sweaters. They made up a sizeable portion of our business.

But they don't wear many sweaters in Florida. We had to find suitable products for the southern market. There were variations in taste in the east, and so we had a whole new variety of regional issues to overcome, making it even more necessary for us to get back on the search to find a chief merchant.

I hired a man who was proposed to us. He had a great record with Burdines, then started Alcutt Andrews, a women's specialty chain. He overexpanded it and went into bankruptcy, but the interview and the people I talked to suggested that he had learned his lesson and was a brilliant merchant who was used to running a company. It appeared that he knew what to do, and I liked him. Earl Harris had met him and pushed me to hire him, which I did.

We had a number of interviews, and one of the things he insisted on was that he had to have authority over all merchandise decisions. He told me that in checking out our company and me he had found that I was very entrenched and made many of the decisions. He was concerned that if he didn't have a clear understanding that it would be his job to make the merchandise decisions, he wouldn't be able to be successful. So he needed a commitment from me that I would stay out of the merchandising and give him a free hand, otherwise he couldn't take the job. I was anxious to proceed; I had been through so many disappointments. Clearly he talked a great game, he was full of ideas, so I made that deal and we shook hands on it.

He came in and took over. The first few weeks, there was some discomfort, but I had made a deal to stay out, and he ran the show. I was glad to be free of the job. As time went on, I observed that he was doing things that I thought were too extreme. He began to make radical choices. He divided each Paul Harris store in two: one side featured red and orange "hot" colors, and the other blue and green "cools." The idea was that when people walked by there would be such a dramatic difference between our store and other stores that they would come in and buy from us. It *was* dramatic. But I worried about alienating our core customers.

He said, "You promised that you would let me do this, and you're going to be satisfied and elated with what we're doing."

We went ahead with his plan. The cool side of the store sold fairly well, but people looked at the hot side of the store, shook their heads, and couldn't quite figure it out. They said, "But I want a pair of black pants, where are they?" We said, "Well, we don't have those. Buy yourself red pants." We started getting into trouble on that mix right away.

At the same time, in the late eighties and early 1990, the retail market began to change. By the fall of 1990, the business began to look grim. The whole retail industry fell into trouble nationally. Consumers were buying less, but because of our optimism, we were gung-ho, despite our dramatic merchandise changes. Industry-wide disappointments were made worse at Paul Harris by yet another bad decision by our head merchant: in his enthusiasm, he decided we could afford to trade up. Trading up meant that, for instance, at Christmas, we would ordinarily sell 20 percent angora sweaters for $29, but he decided we could sell 50 percent angora for $39 or $44. With the Persian Gulf War looming and the economy headed downward, consumers who were used to paying $29 simply did not recognize the additional quality. They weren't interested in paying a higher price for a Paul Harris sweater than they'd paid the year before. This is an example of changes he made in all our lines. Suddenly, we found ourselves having traded up, having optimistically big inventory flow, and customers not buying. We became choked with merchandise and began having problems.

We were overstocked; business was off and we had emergency meetings that ended in taking markdowns in order to reduce inventories and generate cash. Our CFO and I discussed letting our banks know. He felt strongly that he could handle the banks and that I should stay out of it to keep them from becoming nervous. Unfortunately, I did just that. The CFO told the banks we had excess markdowns and would lose money. At the close of a disastrous holiday season, we were not only left with huge overstocks, we had paid more for that merchandise than ever before. We kept marking down goods to create cash, and we had to tell the banks that our losses would be much bigger than we had expected.

Banks were, in general, developing a deep distrust of retail companies; when we reported a much more serious problem than anticipated, they were stunned. Our lenders refused to extend the emergency credit that could have gotten Paul Harris through a very rough season.

February 27, 1991, was the worst day of my career. We had filed

Chapter 11 bankruptcy at court. I went back to the office and called a full meeting in our cafeteria. People knew things were really bad— I'm not sure they expected Chapter 11, but they knew we had serious problems. I called them together and told them. I went on and said that I had every confidence that we could make our way out of this, but we all needed to tighten our belts, grit our teeth, and fight our way out.

The whole prospect was grim. Everyone in the room had to worry: Is my job going to vanish? Will this company still be here in a year? I had worked so hard to develop this staff, bringing people up through the company as we grew. Would they wait around while I figured all this out?

The key executives all stood by me. I said we would keep everybody posted as developments occurred.

At that point, I was close to tears, though I don't think I cried. First one person got up and said, "I believe in Paul Harris and am going to go out and buy stock today." Then several others got up and said, "Yes, I believe in this company, and we're going to get the job done."

We continued talking. People were visibly shaken by all of this, but after I explained that we would work our way through it, they applauded my talk, got up, cheered me, and agreed that it would be tough. They believed in the company.

After all the adversity we'd been through, it didn't seem possible that the current circumstances could bring on the end of our run. Any one of our problems—merchandise mistakes, poor communication with lenders, or a bad turn in the market—could have been managed, the way we'd managed the tornado recovery or the need for new product lines. But the convergence of all those problems in the context of our light-speed expansion had produced results that scared us all. We turned from overconfident and bullish to cautiously tiptoeing ahead, all in one retail season. I knew we could make it. I just didn't know how yet.

We recognized that location was a key factor in reaching our target customers. In the 1970s Paul Harris stores moved from strip shopping centers to the enclosed mall.

This colorful logo reflects the bold styles of the 1970s.

Packaged apparel section in a supermarket in suburban Indianapolis.

Tornado Damage—June 1976

The next season's merchandise would all be destroyed by water damage.

Paul Harris's new construction was completely lost to the storm.

Distribution of merchandise to stores came to a complete halt.

Gerald Paul stands in front of his destroyed construction project, Paul Harris's new distribution center.

COMING
SOON

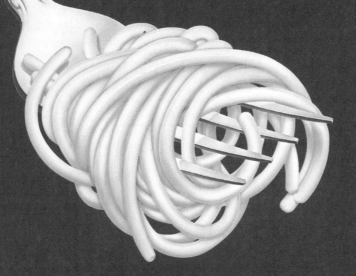

Very Tasty Clothes!

Pasta promotional materials were bright, clever, and geared toward a fun-loving colorful customer.

Pasta selection in a Paul Harris store.

I'm the Paul in Paul Harris

In 1954 Earl Harris and I started this store. Earl's retired now so it's up to me to keep things running right around here.

Of course I can't do everything myself. There's a lot of good people that make this store work every day. I always tell them one thing over and over. I tell them that they don't work for me. They work for you, the customer.

You're the one we have to keep happy. With exciting merchandise. With fair prices. And with service that makes you want to come back. Often.

If there's anything I can do to improve your visits to Paul Harris, you call me personally. And thank you for shopping here. I hope we'll see you more often.

GERALD PAUL
Chief Executive Officer

PAUL HARRIS
Run by the people whose name is above the door.

The Pauls in Paul Harris. This advertising campaign aimed at building an intimate relationship with our customers.

I'm the Paul in Paul Harris too.

I'm Eloise Paul. I've been around retailing all my life. But don't think that because Gerald's my dad I got this job handed to me on a silver platter. Hah!

I started my career working for other stores. In the end I decided that I wanted to work at Paul Harris because there is a commitment to people here.

I learned a lot as I worked my way up in this company. And I made my share of mistakes too. (You've probably seen a few of those on our markdown racks!)

I must say in all honesty, that the clothes we have in the store now are some of the most exciting we've ever put together. If you've liked what you saw don't forget to tell your friends.

ELOISE PAUL
VP of Fashion

PAUL HARRIS
Run by the people whose name is above the door.

Q. Why do we have photos in the store?

A. Photos give the clothing a mood and attitude. They don't need to just be descriptive of the clothes because the real ones right next to the photos do that so much better. What the photo does is show how it "feels" to wear the clothes and what kind of people wear them. It also shows ways to wear them that the customer might not have thought of yet.

Q. Will we always use photography?

A. Photos are very powerful but like everything else that is repeated over and over, you (and the customer) can get used to it. Every once in a while it's more important to communicate some other message, like the giant holly did for Pasta last Christmas.

Publications designed for staff helped them differentiate the Pasta line (left) from the traditional Paul Harris offerings (above).

Gerald Paul Retirement Party

Former employees perform a skit at Gerald Paul's retirement party.

Gerald with his wife, Dorit, and their daughters Allison and Eloise.

CHAPTER ELEVEN

Bankruptcy: A Textbook Recovery

BANKRUPTCY CONSISTS OF A SET OF LAWS designed to help companies and individuals survive financial hardship. There are three types of bankruptcy. We were in Chapter 11. This enabled us to discard a number of leases in poorly performing stores at minimum cost. It enabled us to downsize our operation to a more manageable size and tighten cost controls.

Paul Harris was not the only retail company using the bankruptcy laws to try to establish a firmer footing. The early 1990s found many retail companies operating under bankruptcy protection. Other companies in trouble included Ames Department Stores, Hills Department Stores, Broadway stores, and Florsheim Shoes, to name just a few. The biggest retail bankruptcy belonged to Federated Department Stores, the parent company of Bloomingdale's, which operated under bankruptcy protection for years. Like us, these organizations had ridden the retail high of the late eighties right into the face of the Persian Gulf War, when consumer confidence plummeted amid fears of gas shortages, expensive war spending, and the possibility of losing loved ones in projected ground battles.

There were people who believed that we entered bankruptcy because of poor management. The retailers in bankruptcy in the early nineties were great retailers. They knew what they were doing. Retailing is particularly sensitive to uncontrollable forces in the economy. There are few retailers who have enough cash or access to cash to withstand prolonged downturns. We couldn't simply raise prices to make more money, since the consumer could buy a sweater just like ours in many different places. We had to borrow cash to pay for goods. The borrowing had a cost, which was reflected in the price of the products. In addition to banks, retailers depend a lot on lines of credit from factors. These are companies who work with vendors and pass on the risk of extending credit, for which they charge a fee. At some point when sales are bad, banks and factors refuse to lend you money. While Paul Harris tried to get vendors and manufacturers to lower their prices so that we could charge less and make the same amount of money, we had little leverage.

We had done everything in our power to avoid bankruptcy, but by the 1990 Christmas season, it was obvious that we were going to be out of compliance with some of the covenants that we had made with our three banks. A combination of factors led up to the filing and announcement. Our CFO had thought he could handle the situation, that he could just explain the temporary slowdown in shopping, and he didn't think I should involve myself, that that would make the banks nervous.

The decision to let the CFO take care of the situation turned out to be a big strategic mistake. Our communication procedures had furthered our lenders' mistrust of the retail industry. Our CFO's conviction that he could be our point man with the banks, and that I needn't get involved, gave the impression that my leadership was undisciplined and that *I* was poorly informed. The banks would have preferred to hear the bad news from me.

In December it became clear that we could not pay back all the debt that we had. We had always arranged with the banks that one month out of the year we would not use our credit lines, and that would be right after Christmas, as the stores had just done a third of our annual sales. But as the month went on, inventory was high and our sales were very disappointing. Our margins were declining because we had higher-priced merchandise and had been forced to make unprofitable markdowns in order to bring in enough cash to make payroll and pay bills. We told our board that a serious loss was impending and we felt we had to tell the bank that that was the case. These were very anxious days.

Without huge markdowns we would also have trouble getting out of our Christmas inventory, because after the season ended winter items wouldn't sell well. The damage to our margins turned out to be catastrophic. In January, it was time to explain the forthcoming losses to the banks. We were financed by three separate banks in addition to our loan from Prudential, so the communication of bad news was more complex than for many companies. We had always met all of our obligations and had good relations, so we thought we'd get a slap on the wrist but nothing more serious. Our CFO had told the banks we would have a loss of a few million dollars, but as the weeks in December went on and sales were weak, we cut prices almost daily to create cash and unload inventory. This left us very little margin and even forced us to price merchandise at cost. We had a meeting, and the banks were appalled at the situation. They felt angry that they hadn't been informed about how big a loss we might really have. Moreover, we were unable to give them a final loss estimate, which only exacerbated the situation.

At this point, it became clear that we were going to have a problem. I invited our New York attorneys to send a representative. They sent a junior attorney who was not prepared to deal with the banks' attorneys, and we determined it would be best to hire a top-notch local attorney. We retained Jim Carr from Baker and Daniels. On top of our conflict with local banks, we'd had no communication with Prudential about their twenty-million-dollar loan. They were our largest unsecured creditor, and they had not been kept up to date with any information. When it became apparent that the banks didn't intend to extend our credit, we felt we had better let Prudential know that we had a problem. Prudential was very knowledgeable and sophisticated about retailing. When they got the news of our losses, they felt that their loan was no longer secure, even though we did not owe them any payments yet. They came to a meeting with us and the banks. We had made arrangements to be out of the banks, to pay off our current loans for the thirty-day period in January, as we had always done. Prudential felt that the banks had coerced us into giving them priority.

It was time to bring everyone to the table. We had a meeting attended by me, our CFO, our attorney, and representatives from each of the three banks and Prudential. We presented our situation and were subsequently asked to leave the room.

After waiting for about an hour, we sent someone in to find out what was happening. Prudential had, without our knowing, walked out. The situation became urgent.

We had them paged on the phone at the airport. We asked, "Why did you leave?"

The conversation became heated. They said that they would not take this lying down. They accused us of conspiring with the banks. They had the largest loan and therefore had the most to lose. We had hoped that we could get some covenants to alleviate the crisis, but at this point, Prudential said absolutely no. Then the banks said no, and everyone stopped talking to each other. A battle had begun among our creditors that would greatly damage our chances of regaining our fiscal health. It looked as though our options were running out.

By the middle of January, we needed new merchandise flow. We had this cash crisis, and although Christmas was over, we still had too much inventory. Another meeting was called. When all the people came to the meeting, once again, Prudential walked out.

We thought that since we had a thirty-year relationship with the local banks they would help us through this. But they felt that our CFO had misled them. We presented data of how the company could work its way out and explained the market and the merchandise mistakes that we didn't intend to repeat. Neither the banks nor Prudential believed us. They were looking at our margins for the last year, and we had had all the markdowns to try to get rid of merchandise. They were not inclined to listen to our explanations. As we tried to negotiate a solution, rumors started around the industry that we were in trouble, compounding the situation as suppliers threatened to shut off the flow of merchandise. Without our spring line in stores, we would have no hope of survival.

By early February, our final numbers showed a thirty-million-dollar loss, which was much greater than anyone had expected. It came about as a result of the daily cutting of prices in order to generate cash to pay bills. At that time, both Prudential and the banks said they wanted no more to do with us. This was what brought Paul Harris Stores to the day in February when I filed bankruptcy.

It had never occurred to me that I would be a part of anything like this. To say that I was devastated is putting it mildly; Paul Harris was my life, and it was in danger of failing. I was committed to saving the company and working our way through. I felt everyone in the financial community had let us down, but I also felt challenged to pull the company back together and go forward. After I told everyone at headquarters what had happened, we sent key people out in the field to inform the regional and district managers, hoping no one would have to hear it on the evening news.

Chapter 11 bankruptcy provides legal protection from creditors while a company devises and executes a reorganization plan. A company that fails to get back on its feet eventually closes its doors and liquidates its assets in order to pay as many creditors as possible. Suddenly, I found myself with a company facing grim options. It was a complete turnabout from anything I had anticipated. Those were very dark days. But I was more determined than I'd ever been: Paul Harris would not liquidate.

My highest concern was our employees. People who counted on us would have to be let go in the closing of stores. Further, if we lost our talented, experienced staff, success during and after reorganization would prove incredibly difficult. Our employees faced tough choices: the competition was working hard to recruit our best people away, and staying on was obviously a career risk. Employees working for a company in bankruptcy obviously feel threatened and uncertain. In an effort to show them my commitment, I forced an incentive and bonus package for our employees into the reorganization plan; the creditors opposed it, but I knew a display of confidence was absolutely necessary.

Something extraordinary happened: we didn't lose any key people, turning over only five positions. The people who worked at Paul Harris believed in the company, and they believed in me. They knew that when I said we would make it through, I meant it, that if I had a moment's doubt, I would tell them. Former employees have since said that they were not afraid during the bankruptcy, that they were too busy to worry. They've said that my confidence and drive were contagious. They also knew how much work we had ahead of us and how much they were needed. The relationships a leader builds with employees have many payoffs, but none as clear to me as what happened at Paul Harris during bankruptcy.

Former vice president Jan Woodruff noted a new sense of urgency during the filing. While our creative, entrepreneurial environment helped bring out our employees' best ideas, it seems that the strong sense of direction and the specificity of work during this period was a refreshing, energizing change for some key employees. Their invigoration and renewed commitment were vital but unplanned elements of the company's reorganization.

We went out talking to our people in the field as well, and to this day I feel really good about our retention rate. We'd gone to court to request that special bonuses be provided for key headquarters and field people. I believed that these bonuses were absolutely necessary.

There are certain things you do to preserve a company in bankruptcy. The goal is to trim costs and expenses. The most common way to do this is to eliminate positions. We believed in our people, but as we cut our roster of stores, we had to let people go. This was heart-rending to me. We cared about our people; letting them go was a very bitter pill.

The second way to cut expenses is to eliminate stores that are more costly than profitable. Normally you cannot easily close stores; mall leases make closing stores difficult. However, bankruptcy protection allows an easier option out of leases. We clearly had to close a lot of stores—though exactly how many would be a point of contention for months to come—and go through a process of salvaging the company and getting back to health. There was much to do immediately after the filing in trying to get things together, and it would involve letting people down.

On February 28, the day after filing, another complication began. A man named Ronald Chez, a shareholder from Chicago, decided to buy $125,000 in stock, bringing his total ownership to more than 400,000 shares. He obviously did this for investment reasons as well as hoping to get a strong voice in management decision-making. His investment was a display of confidence in our survival, but also an attempt to gain power. We were acquainted—he had owned stock for some time and would occasionally phone me. His stock purchase and subsequent activity would eventually cause additional complications in our reorganization process.

Dealing with bankruptcy was more than a full-time job. Paul Harris had to operate at its best throughout the process if it was to survive. The merchant whose decisions had contributed to getting us into trouble finally departed, so those responsibilities were all mine again. I was entrenched in merchandise and day-to-day decisions and feared that turning my full attention toward reorganization would leave a gaping hole in the company. Reorganization required weekly financial reporting to each of the three banks and to a creditors' committee headed up by Prudential. I decided to appoint Dale Ball, who was a retired banker and had been working for the company as a computer guru, as VP of Chapter 11. He would handle the complex web of communications that threatened to monopolize my time. Dale was an ex-banker who could speak the banks' language and could instill confidence in the people who were barking at our door.

His task was complicated. The financial reporting we produced each week was various and extremely detailed. Further, the creditors' committee brought in auditors apart from our own national accounting firm, creating another layer of information to manage. Prudential wanted to evaluate whether to do a liquidation analysis, which scared the hell out of me. They wanted to try to get their money back and thought that was the best way to do it. Merely keeping track of the communication each party required was an enormous task. Dale developed an astute information management system, and as a former banker, he understood each party's perspective. He made it possible for me to run the company in the midst of unimaginable chaos. The three banks and Prudential each had accountants and lawyers involved. This was a large group, not always in agreement, whose demands for information had to be satisfied. We were literally under siege from every conceivable area.

One of our first steps was to get key merchants to our vendors to explain that we would work our way out. We asked them to continue to work with us and assured them that the company would get back on its feet. It was essential that we maintain our supply lines if we were to recover. In April of 1991, the Chicago *Tribune* noted, "Despite these problems, Paul Harris has maintained good relations with important suppliers, meaning the stores have remained well-stocked with new spring merchandise," in an article where our situation was called one of "the quieter failures" of a dismal retail era.

Amid all the turmoil, we had to devise a plan that everyone involved—banks, Prudential, shareholders, courts—would approve for paying off our debts and moving into the future. Petrie Stores wrote off an enormous loss on the investment resulting from Milton

Petrie's friendly take-over attempt. On December 30, 1991, we proposed to reimburse each unsecured creditor 100 percent and to divide our reorganized stock with 10 percent to shareholders, 75 percent to creditors, and 15 percent to management. But Ronald Chez and a few other shareholders filed a joint motion to block our proposal. In the face of vehement objections, we returned to the drawing board.

By this time, we had closed 87 stores, nearly a fourth of our company. The creditors' committee had performed its liquidation analysis in the fall with the help of an independent consultant. We spent just over nine million dollars on the expenses of reorganization. Though we were halfway through a profitable fourth quarter, those profits would be eclipsed by the bankruptcy expenses. Things still looked bleak.

In March, we came back to the table with a revised plan. It would involve closing far more stores than we had hoped—almost half our locations—and allocating stock in proportions that did not reward management for their loyalty and effort. Its approval would result in more-than-full repayment of debt. I stood to lose more than anyone: my holding, post-reorganization, was a lean 2.9 percent. After working for most of my life, it was far more important that I'd gotten my company back on its feet.

In August of 1992, Paul Harris emerged from Chapter 11 bankruptcy protection leaner, smarter, and ready to go. We knew more now than we'd ever imagined about running a company in good health and in crisis, and our loyal employees were excited about moving forward. We also had five fresh faces on the board: the reorganization agreement required that our entire board be replaced, with the Prudential-headed creditors' committee in charge of the appointments. Our successful reorganization perked up stock analysts' ears and prompted *Indiana Business Magazine* to name me CEO of the Year in 1994. In the article, stock analyst Raymond H. Diggle, Jr. refers to ours as "a textbook example of how to do Chapter 11 right." We emerged with 201 stores fully operating. We had arranged to pay our creditors 100 percent of what we owed and committed to working with domestic suppliers to allow a faster, more responsive merchandise turnaround. We would begin opening new stores and turning profits within a year and a half.

And finally, our decades-long search for a general merchandise manager had come to a successful end. Eloise Paul, my oldest daughter, had grown up in the company and turned out to be the right person for the job. As we re-merged our Paul Harris and Pasta merchandising divisions, we found that her experience buying for Pasta had prepared her excellently for the direction we would be taking our offering.

I had begun, before the reorganization, to talk about retiring. The board of directors was relieved—they'd begun to worry that I'd hang on forever, leaving no viable successor in my wake. In 1990, I had promised to see the company through its crisis and then begin to disengage. Now it was time to find my replacement. I had run the company for almost four decades. I grew it and saw it through this difficult period and got it back on its feet. I felt it was time for me to depart, and I had no regrets. On the contrary, I looked forward to it.

CHAPTER TWELVE

Passing the Torch

WE EMERGED FROM CHAPTER 11 a lean company with extremely detailed operating guidelines. Our goals were straightforward: we had to manage cash flow very carefully, with weekly reports related to budget planning, benchmarks, and lots of other details; inventory turnover had to become more rapid; the CEO would approve all real estate dealings and marketing strategies; and the company must be concerned above all with making a profit. We were confident that the company would grow again, but for the present, we had to maintain our strict focus in order to operate successfully within our narrow financial means.

As the highest-paid employee, I was the only key executive whose salary hadn't been fully restored to its pre-bankruptcy level. The board and the company instead decided to negotiate an employment contract with me, a move insisted upon by our lender. The bank required that I stay on for one to two more years.

The company had a new financial look following reorganization. The two banks each still owned a bare amount of stock, which they were, of course, free to sell and which subsequently they did sell and turn into a very nice profit. Prudential was the largest shareholder, with 2,850,000 shares, 28 percent of the company's ownership, and I ended up with 680,000 shares, approximately 6.5 percent of the ownership.

We also had a brand-new board of directors, which was appointed by Prudential through their position as chair of our creditors' committee. They interviewed and appointed a number of people of diverse backgrounds, including many in finance, but none who were experts in the various facets of running a retail company. I had worked hard throughout the life of the company to fill out the board with individuals whose contacts and expertise made us better at all the things we did, and this new board, while composed of good people, lacked that dynamic. I had interviewed each new director, and I suppose I could have vetoed the selections, but it didn't seem wise to make the process more complicated. I had also implored Prudential to consider one or two top-notch former directors whose knowledge we had counted on in the past; they honored my wish by interviewing them but did not choose to appoint them to the new board. They didn't want to include anyone from the pre-bankruptcy board.

In this new shape, we tackled the tremendous challenges of getting some meat back on the company's bones. We needed to increase sales and, most importantly, to make a profit. As we gradually succeeded in this, it would put us in a better and more secure position for the future. We had no choice but to move slowly, very cautiously, and to take careful aim at each of our goals. We then began to work on various procedures, ranging from how to run the company to how to merchandise it, and what changes to make. We realized we could not open any stores in the near future because of our limited finances; our whole emphasis was to run the company conservatively, start making a profit, and begin to put our house in order.

I also felt I needed to ingratiate myself with the new board of directors, so that I could convince them to make the right choices as the company moved forward. In essence, I had to sell myself to them. I set about doing this by talking to them about issues in the company and how I thought we should tackle them. Through that process, I could show them that I knew what I was doing and hopefully increase my credibility in their eyes. I met with them individually and learned about each of them. I worked to build a rapport on a personal basis as well; for example, if a director had an interest in art, I'd invite him to our home to see our collection.

Another defining factor drove operational decisions: if we were to take full tax advantage of the forty-million-dollar operating loss we carried forward, we had to conform to an extensive series of guidelines. Of course, the advantage offered by such a significant loss was well worth the extra procedural care it demanded. We structured our post-bankruptcy company around it. It also affected the company's value, which we estimated at seventy million dollars, with ten million shares at seven dollars each. One of the provisions required that no major changes in ownership take place, so we had to work around that as well, despite having set a goal to reduce Prudential's interest somehow. We devoted a huge amount of time to working with our lawyers and accountants in order to stay in compliance.

Meanwhile, as we addressed the demands of our leaner financial capacity and executive operations, we also had to focus on making our stores more effective. We brought in a man named Tom Scott to be the director of stores and make sure that they were running properly, and Eloise had by that time become the general merchandise manager.

William Blair of Chicago, a major financial house and potential underwriter for future stock, interviewed Eloise and issued a report in August 1993. They wrote, "Paul Harris is a turnaround situation and has made significant progress since emerging from Chapter 11. . . . Business trends are showing positive improvement; first half are up 6 percent, total sales are up 7 percent, and operating profit is up substantially, $168,000 vs. $58,000 a year ago. . . . The company sees a gradual increase in average transaction size, which is another positive sign, but we are in a difficult retail environment, and so have to continue to improve."

Eloise basically redirected the merchandise strategy, although as CEO, I was quite involved. She pushed strongly toward coordinated assortments and a singular point of view in the store, and she worked hard on enhancing the company's testing program. She was fanatical about making sure that all the tops and all the bottoms in the store worked together, and that the look they represented was practical for a young working woman on a budget. The emphasis was practicality and easy care. This understanding of what the company needed to stand for to be successful was a more mature incarnation of Eloise's merchandising skills. After the wild Pasta years, we now had to be down-to-earth and practical. The William Blair report went on to say that the company worked on the same concept as Express or The Limited, with a few key items each season, and featuring them was part of the strategy that was developed and which clearly was working. We established a pricing concept that allowed for promotions because the company felt that the core customer liked to buy at reduced prices.

The company then launched an advertising campaign, which emphasized both Eloise and me as "The Pauls in Paul Harris." Large and small signs, including pictures of us and personal messages, appeared throughout the stores.

This campaign attempted to create a more intimate relationship with the customers, something that our competitors like the Limited or Casual Corner could not do, and this proved to be very effective. Generally, the report from the Blair company was very positive.

A year after we emerged from bankruptcy protection, we were clearly making progress, making money, and finding ways to continue to improve and eventually to begin expanding again. We made various projections, including what our financial needs might be. This took up a great deal of our time. As I began to see that this could all eventually work, I also made it clear to employees and to our board that as soon as the company was back on its feet, it was time for me to get out. I had been there for four decades. I was over 65 by then, and I thought we should begin to think about the future CEO.

Rick Bomberger and Rex Steffy both made appeals from within the company for the position. Both had valuable talents, but neither had a head for merchandising. The board worried, too, that the complicated business was too demanding for those candidates, whose work habits we knew well. We would have to go outside of the company to find the next CEO. The board and I discussed this and decided it was the best decision for future leadership.

I pushed to move the recruitment process along. I thought it was time for the company to move forward, and to do that a new CEO with new ideas was required. I felt that I had done my duty long enough.

The board appointed a search committee, of which I was chair, to deal with all the complications of replacing me as CEO. Though I hadn't named a deadline, I insisted that we engage a firm to manage the recruiting process. The committee's first task was to choose that firm and then to evaluate the candidates they provided.

As with the various efforts over the years to find appropriate head merchants, a replacement CEO proved difficult to locate. We engaged Herb Mines, a top-notch retail search firm. They came up with a number of candidates. We trudged through interviews with candidates we didn't want to hire. It's possible that we were gun-shy. I had set out four decades before to build something endur-ing, and I had seen my company almost lost. How could I hand it to someone who hadn't inspired my full confidence?

After ten months, the search firm proposed a woman from Chi-cago named Charlotte Fisher. She had been extremely successful growing Claire's Boutique into an enormous chain. More impor-tantly, she seemed to have what it took to be a leader at Paul Harris. She was dynamic and talked a remarkably good game. Her work history wasn't all positive—she had been fired by Claire's over what was rumored in the industry to be a personality conflict and had failed to save Parklane Hosiery from bankruptcy, but she seemed prepared to learn from failure and be successful.

Instead of making an immediate decision, the search committee proposed to the board to invite Mrs. Fisher to join as a director, so that she could get a deeper feel for the company and we could spend more time with her and observe her.

As a member of the board of directors, she performed well. After approximately six months, the decision was made: Charlotte Fisher was named board vice-chair for a transition period, after which she would assume the role of CEO. I was relieved to be getting off the hot seat—I would be free from the responsibilities of running Paul Harris for the first time in forty years.

Mrs. Fisher would have preferred to skip the transition period, but the board insisted. I agreed to a contract requiring that I stay on for two years as Mrs. Fisher prepared to take over. In the meantime, we were concentrating on making a profit, starting to open stores again, continuing to improve our merchandising, and keeping an eye on our restrictions so that we could make full use of our tax ad-vantages. We were also working on finding a way to get Prudential off being the major shareholder of our company, which we felt was certainly not an advantageous situation. In April of 1997, we had a public offering of three million shares; at that point, Prudential would sell all of its shares, and they made a great profit from their original investment. With that public offering there would be about ten million shares of public stock available. We appeared to be well on our way to a resurgence of strength and growth.

But it became apparent soon after Charlotte Fisher secured the CEO position that we might have made a mistake. Conflicts began to emerge between Mrs. Fisher and key employees. People who had supported her hiring—who still say today that she was the best of the candidates at the time—came into my office, distraught at their new boss's emerging volatility. They described her as a Jekyll and Hyde; she could be charming and articulate one minute, and impossible the next. People came to me and cried. They wanted me to intercede, but I knew that would be wrong.

People who had been dedicated to the company for years began to leave. This new leadership situation was the decision we made, and it wasn't going to change. My office in the company and the contrast between my relationship with employees and hers were only exacerbating a bad situation. I decided it was wrong for me to continue to keep an office at the company, and I had to get out.

My title was chairman emeritus; I decided to move out. I set up an office outside of the company and did some consulting work as well as some public not-for-profit work. I began teaching retail leadership one day a week at Purdue University. I turned my attention away from Paul Harris and toward these new endeavors with the enthusiasm I'd had all my life for learning new things and tried to bring all my years of experience to the advantage of my clients and students. I really enjoyed talking about retailing and the industry and getting students involved and interested. For the first time in my career, I turned my attention away from Paul Harris. I had done everything I could to set the company on the best possible path. For better or worse, my time at Paul Harris was over.

Epilogue

ON JANUARY 20, 1995, WHEN GERALD PAUL left the company in all his capacities, his employees and friends threw a gala retirement party.

The invitation read, "Gerald has built a legacy for Paul Harris Stores of integrity and achievement. Join us for a celebration honoring Gerald and his forty-two years of dedicated leadership at Paul Harris." This, in short form, summarizes the admiration everyone I've met while studying Paul Harris has professed for Gerald Paul.

The party, held at an elegant downtown Indianapolis restaurant, was filled with people from every aspect of the business. Board members, past and present, key Paul Harris managers, and business associates from far and near came to celebrate, including members of the banking and accounting industry, ad agency representatives, and even the principal from Paul Harris's Asian office. The evening was filled with toasts, speeches, and skits. Gerald's employees created an emotional, memorable tribute in their efforts to sum up and celebrate a career so long and filled with accomplishment.

The event launched Gerald Paul into the next phase of his life. As he struggled with the decision to leave the company, he had become disheartened with the direction in which things were moving. The company he built had begun to change. The employee conflicts with the new CEO were having tangible effects: key executives began, one by one, to leave. The company that Gerald Paul had constantly said "was my life" wouldn't survive long after his retirement. Volatility and dicey decision-making drove away people who'd held on through years of evolution, through bankruptcy and recovery. Well past his retirement, he kept tabs on people he'd mentored and brought up in the company, and when they—including his daughter Eloise—left, he called them to express regret for what they'd gone through. Many were surprised and honored. He hadn't been their boss for years by this time, but that didn't seem to matter. Their loyalty was mutual. Gerald was deeply sorry to see the people of Paul Harris unhappy.

This contact with employees was the extent of his involvement with the company. He turned his attention to the benefit of Indianapolis's visual arts organizations, focusing on giving back to the community through volunteerism and support of several area museums. His service to the Indianapolis Museum of Art, the Eiteljorg Museum of Native American Art, the Children's Museum of Indianapolis, and the Indianapolis Art Center have become nearly as legendary in Indianapolis as his career. This service, along with his passion for art collecting, is a direct result of his travels for Paul Harris.

Many of the organizations Gerald has linked himself with are, like him, among the best at what they do. The Indianapolis Museum of Art, where he serves on several committees and chairs the marketing committee, is nationally known for its Asian gallery and its textiles—things Gerald knows more than a little about; the Children's Museum, where he's an active member of the board of directors, is ranked annually as the top in the country. Gerald's wife, Dorit, has served on arts boards and has worked as a docent at the Indianapolis Museum of Art for many years; Gerald's retirement let him join her in these activities.

Gerald's expertise in business and art benefits non-visual arts organizations and programs as well. He's on the board of Ballet Internationale–Indianapolis and an active member of Indiana University's Jewish Studies Program, and he does extremely worthwhile work at Hooverwood Indianapolis Jewish Home. The impulse to give back to the community is common among those successful in business but rarely enacted so completely; service to one or two of the groups to which Gerald is devoted would easily fill the days of the average retired businessman. But service, in all its importance, is only a small part of what Gerald Paul has accomplished in the last ten years.

On June 17, 1998, Purdue University honored Gerald with a doctorate of letters. He donned the traditional cap and gown and, in a full commencement ceremony, marched in the procession to receive his degree from the university's president. He had been devoted in many ways to education throughout his career, seeking participation in studies, peopling his board of directors with professors, and serving on the board of Upper Iowa College. But he had never returned to college himself after giving up his night classes as a young man. The event was a touching surprise and an honor, and also the fulfillment of one of the few goals he hadn't accomplished.

By this time, Gerald was already teaching a retail seminar in Purdue's School of Consumer and Family Sciences. Each fall, he takes on a group of twenty or more students. Instead of a textbook, their coursework is based on experience: Gerald's own, and that of working experts he brings to class each week to talk about their companies and to engage in conversations with the students. Following each class, he takes three different students to lunch, extending the learning environment through informal dialogue. Students say the unusual course structure lets them see another side of the retail industry. For Gerald's part, he gets to stay current and understand the thinking of the young people in his seminars.

And of course, the Pauls have continued to travel, though at their own pace, rather than the fast pace demanded by the company. Leisure travel has included trips—sometimes with children and grandchildren, and sometimes without—all over the world. Destinations like New Zealand, Tahiti, Bora Bora, Vietnam and Cambodia, Istanbul, the Black Sea, and many cities in Europe have continued to be educational experiences, with occasional visits to apparel manufacturers and continuing his art collecting in many cities. On one extraordinary trip, the Pauls introduced their daughters and grandchildren to the cities they called home before leaving Nazi Germany. In Witten, where Gerald was born, the family was received in grand fashion by the town's mayor. The local government had a representative who was in touch with many Jewish families who had fled, and had arranged the special visit. The mayor gave the children gifts and celebrated the Pauls. The family then visited Mannheim, where Dorit had lived. The children were disappointed because the mayor hadn't come out, but the family was able to return to the house where Dorit had lived, getting a glimpse of a part of their origins.

Gerald's post-retirement travel also included a consulting trip to Russia for an organization called the Citizens Democracy Corps. The organization, established to encourage capitalism in formerly communist regions, worked as a nonprofit to provide resources to businesses in Central and Eastern Europe. They contacted Gerald to help an apparel manufacturer in Nizhny Novgorod, a provincial city of about 1.5 million. The company was seeking funding to expand its operation; Gerald's job was to advise the company on its current operations and make a recommendation to CDC to approve or decline the funding request.

During three weeks in Nizhny, Gerald and Dorit stayed in a small apartment, working all day. Gerald was picked up each morning and dropped off at night; Dorit put her many years of museum experience to work, visiting art museums and giving presentations. She has remained in contact with the Russian museums and helped to foster relations with American museums. The company Gerald visited did receive funding, and Gerald spent time at local universities talking to business students. This was a different Russia from the country the Pauls had visited during the Soviet Union's reign. The company's principals had been academics; the business students in the universities were passionate about learning to be entrepreneurs and open their own businesses. Fledgling capitalism had presented itself to them as opportunity; they were not unlike how Gerald had been in 1954.

All of these components, of course, add up to a life incredibly well-lived. People say that we make art, have children, and build businesses in some kind of quest for immortality, as an effort to outlive our bodies. It's possible that what you make, when you build something, is nothing more or less than an extraordinary life— which may, after all, be the best that anyone can do.

But when you build an organization like Paul Harris, you touch other people, too. The culture of entrepreneurship, energy, and exchange at Paul Harris changed people's lives. We spend far more waking time working than doing anything else in our daily lives. So many people who worked at Paul Harris had found their dream job and, years later, still hold it close to their hearts. In 2002, many of them got together for a reunion; they were, after all, a family in so many ways.

Paul Harris Stores, Inc. closed its doors for the last time in 2001.

By then, Gerald Paul hadn't been a part of it for years. Someone runs five stores in Indiana that bear the name Paul Harris, having bought the name in a bankruptcy proceeding, but they have nothing to do with the company Gerald built. Does it mean anything that Paul Harris Stores, Inc. didn't survive long past his retirement? That depends on whom you ask. Gerald is confident that he did everything in his power to ensure the company's longevity. He used the same forward-thinking decision-making process that had carried Paul Harris so far in picking a successor and considering the company's future. This one last time, it failed him.

But it seems, from an outsider's perspective, as if the company really was Gerald Paul; he was, in some intangible way, indispensable. Former employees have told me that when they left the company, a prospective employer's culture drove their decisions about where they might go next. They describe Gerald as the quintessential entrepreneur and say that there's no better definition of *entrepreneurial* than the story of Paul Harris and of Gerald's life. The qualities they've looked for in employers aren't quite concrete, but seem to center around the word *culture*. Some, unable to find the opportunities for growth and creativity they had at Paul Harris, have left the retail industry altogether.

For others, Gerald's mentorship, the growth they experienced, and the accomplishments they piled up have helped prepare them for ongoing success. Former Paul Harris employees teach at major universities, work in organizations all over the city and country, and have started their own businesses.

As for Gerald, he's going to keep seeing the world, working to promote the arts, and teaching the next generation of retail innovators. He is in demand in his hometown, where arts organizations extend regular invitations to meetings, events, and parties, where businesspeople call on him to consult with their firms. He'll keep going to Mexico with his family each Christmas and to a fitness spa at Canyon Ranch in Tucson, Arizona each spring, always learning, always growing.

—Victoria Barrett

Dec18/07